Kerry O'Sullivan speaks German, Farsi, Indonesian, Russian, Dutch and Thai, in addition to his native English. A highly qualified language teacher and interpreter/translator, during a twenty-year period he has lived and worked in Thailand, Holland, England, Switzerland, Iran, Yugoslavia, the USA, Indonesia and Hong Kong.

He holds degrees in applied linguistics and languages and has worked as a senior lecturer in Linguistics at Macquarie University and as a principal lecturer at the Hong Kong Polytechnic. He has also served as Director of the Australian Language Centre and as a senior aid expert and World Bank consultant.

UNDERSTANDING WAYS
Communicating between cultures

Kerry O'Sullivan

HALE
& IREMONGER

DEDICATED, AS ALWAYS, TO

MAS AND MOS

Design and layout by
Superkern Desktop,
18 Mitchell Street, North Sydney, NSW
10 9 8 7 6 5 4 3

Illustrations by
Jason Cameron

Printed and bound by
Southwood Press Pty Limited
80–92 Chapel Street, Marrickville, NSW

For the publisher
Hale & Iremonger Pty Limited
GPO Box 2552, Sydney, NSW

National Library of Australia Cataloguing-in-publication entry

O'Sullivan, Kerry, 1952- .
    Understanding ways: communicating between cultures.

    Bibliography.
    ISBN 0 86806 537 4.

    1. Intercultural communication. I. Title
303.482

Cover illustration and design: T. E. Tan

CONTENTS

3

What are you trying to say?
Looking at communication   59

4 Developing the right skills
Managing intercultural communication 97

Acknowledgements

My first and greatest thanks go to Sue Benson for her
energy, skill, and commitment to this project.

I would also like to acknowledge and thank Professor Christopher
N. Candlin and Ken Willing, both of Macquarie University, for
inspiring me through their teaching and writing, and Jean Brick,
Dr Rebecca Bradley and Dr Robin Thelwall for encouraging me
and sharing so much with me over the years.

Personal thanks also go to Martin Sitompul,
Mavis O'Sullivan, and Joyce Gisler.

ABOUT THIS BOOK

A number of explanations and cautionary notes need to be made about this book:

- The book's style and content inevitably reflect my own culture, although I have tried to minimise this. It is unlikely that anyone can think, speak, or write in a culture-neutral way. I can only note the existence of bias and ask for your understanding.

- Examples in the book are drawn from a range of research studies and from my own intercultural experience. As such, they do not cover, in any deliberately balanced way, the full range of cultures found in the world.

- The usual caution should be exercised with regard to the research studies referred to in the book. Exactly what questions were researched? Was the research really examining what it claimed to be examining? In what populations and at what time was the research conducted? What methodology was used, and are the results reliable? I have provided references for each study if you would like to examine them further.

- The common convention of using the word 'America' to refer to the United States (and 'Americans' to its people) is followed throughout the book. It should be noted, of course, that the term 'America' actually refers to the entire American continent.

- My culture (and some other English-speaking cultures) have become increasingly concerned about avoiding language that favours one sex over the other. When I have used forms of 'he' or 'she', I hope that this will not be seen as favouring or referring exclusively to one gender.

- My ideas, interpretations and analyses throughout the book should be regarded for what they are — personal opinions only. In matters of culture and intercultural communication, there are no definitive clear-cut answers.

Worm and crow experiencing cultural exchange

The way we do things around here
Understanding the basics of culture

1

TWO questions. What does 'culture' mean to you? And why should you bother about improving your communication with people from other cultures?

You may not be very aware of culture in your day-to-day life. Maybe you become aware of it only when it becomes 'visible': for example, when you work with somebody from another culture; or manage a multicultural office; teach a class of students from different cultural backgrounds; talk to a neighbour from another culture; take an international vacation; go on a business trip; or deal with foreign clients.

Through these contacts, you may have become more aware of difference and begun to see 'culture' as a significant force which brings not only interest and enjoyment, but also perhaps difficulty, discomfort, or even conflict. Something *new* needs to be managed.

This book is about managing intercultural contact, acquiring the knowledge, awareness, and skill to communicate successfully across cultures. Once acquired, this knowledge, awareness and skill can be used in *any* contact situation — from the neighbourly chat to the international business meeting — and with *any* culture. The aim of the book is not to teach you about any one particular culture, but rather how to manage *all* intercultural interactions.

The book does not aim to make you a 'better' (more open-minded, more tolerant) person. If, after you learn more about the astonishing diversity of ways of seeing, being, behaving, and communicating in the world, you do feel more open-minded and more tolerant, that's great — but it is not the aim of this book.

Nor does this book ask you to change your culture. Why should you? And, anyway, how many of us could change our culture even if we wanted to? After 25 years 'on the road', living and working in many different cultures, I am still recognisably Australian in culture.

Nor does it ask you to like all aspects of all cultures; is that realistic? It does encourage you, however, to acknowledge the validity of other cultures.

- ✘ The aim is to become a better, more tolerant person.
- ✔ The aim is to become a more skilled intercultural communicator.
- ✘ You need to learn to accept and like other cultures.
- ✔ You need to respect the validity of other cultures.
- ✘ You have to change your culture.
- ✔ There is no reason to change your culture.

SO, WHAT IS 'CULTURE' THEN?

How would you define 'culture'? Having considered the issue yourself, here are a few definitions to consider:

> It refers to all the accepted and patterned ways of behavior of a given people. It is a body of common understanding. It is the sum total and the organization or arrangement of the group's ways of thinking, feeling, and acting... In this sense, of course, every people has a culture and no individual can live without culture. It is our culture that enables us to get through the day because we and the other people we encounter attach somewhat the same meanings to the same things. (*Man and Culture*, Ina C. Brown)

> Culture is that complex whole which includes knowledge, belief, art, morals, law, customs and other capabilities or habits acquired by members of a society. (E.B.Taylor)

> The sum total of ways of living built up by a group of human beings, which is transmitted from one generation to another. (*The Macquarie Encyclopedic Dictionary*)

> The way we do things around here. (A student in Thailand)

Do any of these definitions match your own? Whichever you choose, we are clearly dealing with something large and pervasive. Culture is not just a matter of what we eat, what we wear, and how we sing and dance.

My own definition of culture is '*the ways people agree to be*'. Over periods of time groups of people (societies) reach agreements about how they see the world, how they will behave, interact with each other, judge each other, organise themselves, manage themselves, and so on — in other words, how they will exist, how they will *be*. Naturally, these agreements are usually unstated and unconscious: we learn the agreements — the 'rules' — as part of growing up in our societies. We internalise them and they become automatic. We become conscious of them only when we come into contact with another group whose rules are different.

What culture do you belong to? A word of caution: your 'culture' is not necessarily the same as your 'nationality' and 'ethnicity'. We need to be clear about the difference.

In some cases, all three may be the same. Take for example 'Lek'.

● Lek regards herself as culturally Thai, she holds Thai citizenship, and she is ethnically Thai (that is, she belongs to that group of people whose physical appearance we recognise as Thai. Even if some people have difficulty in distinguishing her from a Korean or a Japanese, she and her fellow Thais would have little hesitation in making the distinction.).

The case is often, however, far more complex. Consider another person I know.

- Mei-Ling was born and grew up in Beijing, speaking Putonghua (Mandarin). At the age of 14, she and her family moved to Hong Kong, where she learnt Cantonese and later attended university. At the age of 27, she migrated to Canada, where she ultimately married a French Canadian from Quebec and became a citizen. As her children grew up and as she settled into her job and improved her English, she became increasingly comfortable with the way of life in Canada, although she still retains what she regards as her Chinese-ness. Her daughter Cindy was born in Toronto. She speaks English as her first language and (through her French father) is reasonably fluent in French. She speaks only a few words of Mandarin. She is very interested in the Chinese and French cultures, particularly when she sees her grandparents, but overall she sees herself as a Canadian, no different in her attitudes and behaviour from most of her classmates.

Of course the key is *self*-image, *self*-identification. How do you see yourself? Your nationality will probably be quite straightforward, as is your ethnicity (although this will be open to your own interpretation), but what about your culture? Suppose a passport required you to describe not only your nationality, but also your ethnicity and your *culture*. What would you say?

- ✗ Culture and ethnicity are the same.
- ✗ All people holding the same nationality will have the same culture.
- ✅ Culture, nationality and ethnicity are distinct concepts.
- ✅ Know what culture you belong to.
- ✅ Don't make assumptions about people's culture based on their ethnicity or nationality.

Labels describing people can be problematic, as we see when we compare the following:

- Terms such as 'American', 'Nigerian', 'South African', 'Malaysian', 'Australian', and 'Venezuelan' can refer to nationality and culture, but not to ethnicity.

- 'Balinese', 'Navajo', 'Hawaiian' may be used to refer to culture and ethnicity, but they are not nationalities. 'Russian' and 'Lithuanian', on the other hand, could until recently only refer to ethnicity and culture — but now they are also nationalities.

- 'Japanese', 'German', and 'Thai', however, can refer to all three concepts (which of course does not necessarily mean that all *nationals* of these countries identify themselves as ethnically and culturally Japanese, German or Thai).

If you are feeling a little confused, you are not alone. Governments and social institutions — and of course ordinary people in their daily lives — often engage in redefining themselves or reasserting their identity. They may use physical appearance, clothes, language (or accent), point of residence, religion, or some other intangible as the critical factor in defining themselves and others. Ultimately, there is no objective way of deciding someone's ethnicity or culture. What they decide for themselves is the answer.

Another distinction that needs to be made is between 'culture' and 'lifestyle'. The two concepts can overlap. For the sake of clarity, let's restrict 'lifestyle' to those physical aspects of our lives which are readily visible and which are not generally sources of intercultural miscommunication. Aspects of lifestyle, therefore, would include food (that is, *what* we eat, not *how* we eat it, or *how we feel* about it, both of which are aspects of culture) and clothes (again, *what* we wear, not *what we believe* to be appropriate, polite, etc. with regard to our clothing, which are clearly cultural decisions).

Issues of lifestyle are not considered in this book. We are concerned here with the less visible things: attitudes, beliefs, values, behaviour, and communication.

One point about 'lifestyle' needs to be made, however. The twentieth century has seen a steadily increasing convergence in some aspects of lifestyle, especially among young urban dwellers. Greater similarities now exist across cultures in relation to preferred clothing, consumer goods, music, and even — to some extent — food. These superficial similarities can tend to mislead people into thinking there is a convergence in culture, which is not necessarily the case at all. I can eat French bread, listen regularly to French music, and adopt the latest French fashions, but this doesn't mean I am French in culture or that I can understand French culture.

- Culture and lifestyle are not the same thing.
- Don't draw conclusions about a person's culture based on some aspect of their lifestyle.

How would you regard yourself in terms of ethnicity, nationality, and culture? Are there any aspects of your lifestyle that have come from other cultures?

WHY BOTHER ABOUT CULTURE?

There may be different reasons why you might be interested in developing intercultural communication skills. Perhaps:

- You feel we *should* do it, for the sake of improved understanding and harmony. It is a worthy goal in itself.

- You feel that you *need* to do it if we are going to be successful in interacting with one other, doing business with one another and living together successfully. It is a means to an end.

- You *want* to do it for its own sake. It is an enjoyable and self-enriching goal.

You will know which of these descriptions best fits your own motivation, or perhaps you are motivated by all three.

The important point to note is that, regardless of the motivation, the process of developing intercultural awareness and skills is basically the same.

Although it is difficult to quantify, governments, business leaders, educators and other professionals increasingly testify to the impact of intercultural *mis*communication on efficiency, productivity, and effectiveness in education, commerce, and international relations. It means money lost and opportunities lost. In other situations, such as international travel or where different cultures live together in the one society, the emotional effects of poor intercultural communication can range from discomfort through anxiety to open conflict. The stakes can be high.

Conversely, the benefits from improved intercultural communication are considerable. Potentially they include greater effectiveness and efficiency, and — in emotional terms — perhaps (although not automatically) greater personal development.

What is the way forward? Maybe, as cultures come into more contact in the modern world (the 'global village'), people will become more experienced, and intercultural understanding will emerge naturally. Unfortunately, we know from extensive research[1] and from our own experience, that increased contact *alone* does not lead to improved communication, contrary to the belief and hopes of many people. In fact, increased contact can make the situation worse.

What about goodwill? If we all make a collective effort to be open-minded and tolerant and sensitive — to be *nice* to one another — all will be well. This is a good start, but it will not get us very far. It is like saying that we can become good drivers if we wish it to be so: don't worry about understanding the controls of a car or the rules of the road, and don't worry about practising the skills of competent driving. Just have the right attitude and all will be well. Unfortunately, it doesn't work that way.

There must be more — and there is. As with any other area of human competence, there are elements of attitude, awareness, knowledge, and skill which are necessary to improve intercultural communication.

- If we have more contact, intercultural understanding will improve.
- Goodwill and tolerance are all you need to be successful in intercultural communication.

◍ Goodwill and tolerance provide a reasonable start, but they are not enough.

◍ Look for the knowledge, awareness and skill needed to improve intercultural communication.

How do we begin? The first step in developing those skills is to extend our awareness of cultural difference.

How different are cultures from one another? A difficult question, perhaps like asking 'How long is a piece of string'? Here is my answer: *the differences are probably wider and deeper than most of us imagine.* As you read this opinion, you may disagree. You may even be a little annoyed or offended. You feel that 'underneath' we are all basically the same, and that if only we were more tolerant and sensitive, we could overcome any superficial differences. In turn, I would say that you are probably reflecting the attitudes of your particular culture to this issue — and, incidentally, I can probably guess which culture you belong to! It is one of the characteristics of your culture that you feel that all people are fundamentally similar.

If, on the other hand, you feel that cultures are so different that successful intercultural communication is impossible, then this too is unacceptable. No matter how problematic, it cannot be denied that intercultural communication has been succeeding for centuries and is succeeding today — no matter how awkwardly.

If, however, the view is expressed in another way — namely, that (a) the people of all cultures face the same fundamental dilemmas of life, that (b) all cultures are valid and worthy of respect, and that (c) cultures are capable of successful interaction — then I have no major difficulty. This stance allows for the reality of enormous diversity and provides a basis for progress.

✖ Underneath, people are fundamentally the same.

◍ Underneath, the people of the world can be profoundly different.

✖ Cultures are so different that we will never be able to communicate successfully.

◍ People have always succeeded and they will continue to succeed in intercultural communication.

◍ Accept cultural difference as a reality.

Before we look at the issue of cultural difference, we first need to check a few basics, just in case there are any misunderstandings.

WE ALL HAVE RITUALS

We begin the long process of 'learning' our native culture very early in life. Children as young as five can distinguish ethnicity (although the ability to distinguish cultural difference comes much later and remains less conscious).

Throughout childhood and adolescence, we develop specific ways of behaving, thinking and communicating. We do this by unconsciously observing and modelling ourselves on our parents, siblings, friends, teachers, neighbours, even film and literary characters. Our progress is monitored, praised and criticised along the way, leading to reinforcement or adjustment. As an example, consider for a moment how parents in your culture teach children appropriate requesting behaviour (handing a child a gift, the parent may ask 'What do you say?'). How do they praise or correct the child's response? The child is being taught its native culture (how to behave appropriately).

The process of learning our native culture takes longer than learning our native language, and is probably not 'complete' until adulthood. (This is, of course, a common source of stress between adolescents and parents, who — in most cultures — continue to impose constraints on their pre-adult children, precisely because they feel that their cultural education is not yet complete, even if the children feel that it is!)

Our cultural behaviour becomes so natural and so programmed that we sometimes tend to think that only other cultures have rituals and customs. ('Oh, isn't that quaint, interesting, strange?') We are prepared to regard Papua New Guinea Highlanders or Balinese as having rituals, but 'we' don't. Similarly, other people may have 'tribes', but somehow we don't. To remind us of this point, I often use the term 'tribe' throughout this book, simply referring to a group of people with the same culture.

Because our own cultural behaviour is usually quite automatic and unconscious, we tend not to think of it as cultural behaviour! To illustrate this, read the following description of a ritual. As you read it, decide what kind of ritual it is and in which tribe it might take place:

- This ritual can occur at any time of the year: there is no particular fixed date for it. It usually starts during the daytime and often extends late into the night. Participation in the ritual is not open to everyone: only some members of the tribe are permitted to take part in one of these rituals. These participants do unusual things to 'enhance' their appearance. Some wear paint on their faces and some put an oily substance in their hair. Some participants artificially increase their height by the use of specially-made devices under their feet: this is considered by most people in the tribe to look attractive. Cowskin and cloth are worn by most of the participants, although small amounts of metal can also be seen. The key ceremony during the ritual revolves around a small group of participants who repeat sacred words assisted by a holy man. During this part of the ritual, the other participants are expected to listen quietly, but upon its completion, they are encouraged to throw a special kind of food at the

7

small group, especially at the man and the woman who appear to be the main focus of the ritual. The significance of this food-throwing has not been determined, but some researchers believe that it is connected with fertility. The remainder of the ritual, which can last for many hours, is conducted in a separate location. The main focus of this part of the ritual appears to be the drinking of fermented liquids, although a number of other activities also take place. Researchers are not in agreement as to the purpose and meaning of these activities.

How quickly did you realise that you were reading a description of a Christian wedding, as conducted in, say, England or Australia?

Of course not all rituals are quite as formalised as a wedding, but they are nevertheless rituals. Consider, for example, your behaviour at a party. What will you do when you arrive, how will you greet the people you know, what will you talk about, how will you get to know the people you haven't met before, what will you do at the party, what will you say when you want to leave the party? Although the answers may vary slightly from person to person in your tribe, there will be a very strong similarity among your tribe's answers. This is because you share the same 'script' for this ritual.

Now compare your script with another tribe's. Here is the script for the Indonesian tribe (of course, allowing for the usual diversity within any tribe):

- When I arrive, I will go around to every person at the party and shake hands with them. I will smile and say my name and then move on to the next person. When I have done the rounds, I can relax and chat with whomever I want to. After we eat (and the host will make sure that this happens at the appropriate time), one or more of the guests — usually people with more senior status — will tell the host that they have to leave (generally by saying 'it's already late'). The host will urge them to stay. We will then all immediately follow suit, thanking the host as we leave (who will, again, urge us all to stay).

Naturally we all have the option of breaking these patterns and refusing to conform, but this break will be seen as strange, rebellious, impolite, or 'anti-social'.

Of course we may not be aware that we are breaking the pattern: this is often the case with children (who still need to learn the rules).

If, however, adults are *unaware* they are not conforming, they will usually be regarded as having a personality problem or a mental health problem.

Of course, cross-culturally we often do not follow the rules, either because we are unaware of them or because we choose not to, even if we are aware of them. How will this be interpreted? The good news is that, fortunately, most tribes will not think we have a mental illness if we don't conform to their rules. Nor of course will they assume we are children. The bad news is that they will often think our behaviour is strange or impolite. They measure us against *their* standards (perhaps the only ones with which they are familiar).

We all have a tendency to take things for granted and assume that our standards are normal and universal. Avoiding taking things for granted — stepping outside your behaviour and seeing that your behaviour is determined by your specific culture — is the base requirement for successful intercultural communication.

- ✖ Other cultures have customs and rituals. We don't.
- ✖ Other people may follow customs and rituals. I don't.
- ✖ I can do exactly what I want. My actions are independent of my culture.
- ✔ Quite a lot of my behaviour is ritualised. It follows a pattern prescribed by my cultural group.
- ✔ I don't have total freedom of choice in my behaviour.
- ✔ My actions are rule-governed.
- ✔ Accept that you are a member of a culture which regulates your behaviour.

CULTURES ARE VERY DIFFERENT FROM ONE ANOTHER

Perhaps one of the most interesting and important cultural differences we can see is the variety of attitudes that cultures hold to cultural difference itself! Which do you believe?

- 'Underneath, we are all fundamentally similar'; or
- 'We are fundamentally different.'

Remember your answer to this question is probably largely determined by your culture!

To help you answer the question, ask yourself whether it is possible for an outsider to become a member of your tribe. If it is possible, what adjustments or what circumstances would need to occur before that outsider is included?

Here are some responses to this question from people in different tribes:

- 'We Americans... believe only in the superficial differences between the peoples of the world.'[2]

Here is another answer, this time about Australian culture and Chinese culture:

- 'Australians tend to believe that people everywhere are basically Australian. Cultural differences are seen as superficial and that, underneath, people really behave as Australians do. Newcomers (to Australia) are therefore expected to conform to the Australian way of life. Failure to do so can be taken as evidence of hostility. Most Chinese, on the other hand, tend to believe that a non-Chinese is different from a

Chinese in a way that is almost impossible to overcome. So people are surprised when a non-Chinese speaks fluent Chinese or when they express an appreciation for something felt to be typically Chinese. Such appreciation may be interpreted as an unusual display of friendship or solidarity while a lack of adaptation is more to be expected and not necessarily indicative of hostility.'[3]

And yet another, discussing the acceptance into a Central American tribe of an outsider:

- 'She was unhesitatingly accepted by the people, who did not require that she disavow her own culture, only that she integrate the new material into what was already there.'[4]

Here is an Australian journalist writing about a university graduation ceremony in Sydney, in which he notes the ethnic mix of the graduates and the particular success of the 'Asian' students:

- 'Good luck for next year to the Nguyens and the Phus, the Phimsipasoms and the Vongsayasys, the Cheungs and the Ngothans. They're good Australian names.'[5]

Finally, try this as a test. Is it possible for me, Kerry O'Sullivan, a white Australian (ethnically Celtic), to become a member of your tribe if I do my utmost to learn your language and culture?

Are there universals of behaviour? Clearly, there are universal *categories* of behaviour. One pioneer researcher claimed five 'panhuman cultural categories', each with a number of sub-categories, yielding a total of 73 universals in all. The inventory comprised:

- *individual behaviour* (comprising 8 categories, including bodily adornment, personal names, gestures, hair styles, mourning)

- *social behaviour* (comprising 12 categories, such as dancing, gift giving, hospitality, games, joking, visiting, kinship naming)

- *social control and education* (comprising 27 categories, including marriage, law, property rights, sexual restrictions, status differentiation, inheritance rules, education, government, modesty concerning natural functions)

- *technology* (comprising 15 categories, such as calendars, cooking, toolmaking, trade, numerals, obstetrics, medicine)

- *collective beliefs* (comprising 11 categories, including dream interpretation, religious ritual, propitiation of supernatural beings, magic, religious ritual).[6]

Note, however, that no claim is made for the *same* behaviour in each of these, only that *each exists in every culture*.

To get you into your own examination of cultural difference, consider the following. In your opinion, does culture influence the way people do the following?

- greet each other?
- react to a compliment?
- apologise?
- watch t.v.?
- regard sexual behaviour?
- dismiss employees?
- interview applicants?
- assess their status in society?
- stand when talking to the boss?
- define friendship?
- make small talk?

The answer in all cases is 'yes'. While there will be easy agreement on some items, others may require some discussion.

Take 'reacting to a compliment', for example. Here some of the culture-specific alternatives include: (i) modestly demur, (ii) accept the compliment and thank the speaker, (iii) laugh and dismiss the compliment, (iv) state that the opposite of the compliment is the case.

What about 'watching t.v.'? Here some of the culture-specific alternatives include (for a group of people watching together): (i) sit quietly (discuss later or during the commercials) or (ii) discuss and comment as you watch. Other differences will occur in, for example, preferred levels of volume and brightness, or even in viewing 'style', for example to what extent the viewers use anticipation while viewing.

And what about 'talking to the boss'? Some of the options here are hands in front or behind, clasped or open; body straight or inclined.

Finally, 'friendship' will vary according to who is included based on what criteria; the degree of familiarity required to be defined as friend (as opposed, for example to an 'acquaintance', if indeed such a concept exists), and so on.

It can easily be argued that 'culture' is pervasive, influencing virtually all aspects of our behaviour and communication:

- Culture influences who made your breakfast, whether you live at home with your parents or not, how you greeted your spouse/family members this morning, how you parted from your spouse/family members when you left for work, whether and how you prayed this morning, how you feel about your job, how other people regard your job, what items you have on and near your desk or in your office, how you greeted your co-workers when you arrived at work this morning, how you call your superiors, peers, and subordinates, the first thing you said when seeing your boss today, how you answer the telephone, how you ask to speak to someone on the telephone, how you behave in meetings, your posture when the boss walks past, the kinds of things you are trying to show about yourself in meetings (I have good ideas, I'm very supportive, I'm really paying attention, etc.), the way you write memos, the way you write business letters, what you think about women (men) working in your field, how you relate to co-workers who are younger, older than you, how you make suggestions to other workers, how you criticise the work of others, how you apologise, which things you feel you should apologise for and which ones not, when you feel it's appropriate to interrupt somebody and how you do it, how you explain absence or lateness, how you get other people to help you, when you feel it's appropriate to admit that you are wrong and how you do it, what you think about things you read in the newspaper, what you chat about with people, how you act when you meet people for the first time, what you do to persuade someone, how you regard the quality of your work and the quality of other people's work, what you believe is polite behaviour, how you feel, your concept of happiness, the way you express anger, what you think will happen to you when you die, who you will marry, how many children you (are planning to) have, how you console people, how you ...

- ✖ Culture is superficial.
- ✖ Culture is confined to behaviour.
- ✖ Underneath, people are fundamentally the same.
- ✔ Culture is pervasive.
- ✔ Culture influences the way people act, see, feel, do, interact, judge.
- ✔ Underneath, the people of the world can be profoundly different.

CULTURES ARE NOT FIXED — THEY CHANGE OVER TIME

Of course, the rules of a culture keep changing, gradually in some cases and very rapidly in others. Sometimes, the changes are almost imperceptible, without any particular attention focused on them. The change is incorporated into the group's 'constitution' without any fuss. Sometimes, the change comes very openly and is subject to widespread discussion and debate.

Our societies are always subjecting at least some of the rules to scrutiny, either deciding to reconfirm them, to adjust them, or to overturn them. We rage, debate, discuss in whatever forums are available to us — the town hall meeting, the argument around the well, letters to the editor, the chat during dinner, the television program, the election campaign, the village meeting — deciding, either explicitly or implicitly, what directions the 'tribe' should take, constantly redefining what is good, what is appropriate, what is wise.

Here is just one example, taken from Singapore. In this example, the writer is reacting to a letter-to-the-editor written by a Mr Stanley Cheung. The topic is appropriate cultural behaviour in the workplace and the writer argues for a reaffirmation of traditional cultural values and a rejection of introduced foreign values.

> Stanley Cheung presented an interesting observation on employer/ employee relationships in both a Chinese and non-Chinese context. In his view, a more rewarding work environment is where the boss is referred to on a first name basis. Mr Cheung ought to know this is unthinkable, not only in the workplace but in a Chinese home. Appropriate terms of respect are used to address every family member. A twin brother or sister may only be a few minutes older, but he or she would still have to be addressed (in Mandarin) as ge ge or jie jie. In an office you would have to use the same kind of deference… The average Chinese company has not lost out to any Western contemporary whose productivity depends on a 'hail-fellow-well-met' attitude. (Letter to the Editor, *Asia Magazine*, 8 May 1993: [Chan Kwee Sung, Singapore.])

Sections of a particular culture (perhaps some of the women of the society or some of its young people or its government) can make enormous changes to certain aspects of the culture. Cultures such as those of the United States and Australia, for example, underwent quite dramatic changes in the 1960s — both in attitudes and behaviour. Indeed, we can see that the whole concept of 'generation gap' is of course an expression of cultural change. The 'rules' keep changing.

If your tribe has seen the widespread introduction of television and telephones in recent decades, what changes in cultural behaviour can you see having resulted from these innovations?

Has your tribe adopted any of the following agreements in the last, say, ten to twenty years? 'It is reasonable for a man and a woman to live together without being married.' 'Women can become engineers.' 'People shouldn't smoke indoors.' 'Young people should choose their own marriage partners.' 'We can't just keep using up our forests.'

✖ Cultures are fixed forever.

✔ Cultures are constantly changing.

CULTURES ARE NOT UNIFORM — THEY VARY INTERNALLY

In all cultures — even those that outwardly appear to be very homogeneous — there can be tremendous diversity.

This diversity can be due to many factors: age; differences in education within the society; differing perspectives or behaviour associated with different class or status in the society; and the development of new perspectives by sections of the society, to name just a few.

Clearly, the diversity within a culture is one of the engines that drives cultural change. A totally homogeneous society would not change unless through outside influence.

It is extremely important to recognise diversity within tribes. In describing a culture, we can really only speak in terms of generalisations and tendencies, trying to identify the typical or representative characteristics of a people.

In the following situations, does your tribe encourage or require uniform behaviour, or does it allow a wide range of alternatives?

1. behaviour at a funeral
2. residence after marriage
3. duration of education undertaken
4. behaviour and dress of widows
5. courtship behaviour
6. responses to receiving a gift
7. behaviour in a job interview

For my tribe, I would say that the range of options is very limited in situations #1, 6, and 7. For example, when I receive a gift I need to (i) express my gratitude, (ii) express my liking for the gift (regardless of how I actually feel), and (iii) depending on the circumstances and occasion, tell the gift-giver that they 'shouldn't have' bought the gift. In the other situations (#2, 3, 4, and 5) the choice is relatively open.

Within cultures we have 'subcultures' — smaller groupings based on a range of factors such as wealth, education, interests and pastimes, profession, religion, marital or parental status, area of residence, region of origin, way of speaking (dialect), and so on. What *sub*cultures do you belong to?

These factors influence our self-identity and may influence our communication and behaviour. Yet, at some level, the subcultures share a bedrock of cultural similarity (no matter how much they may resist that view!). I would say, for example, that a rebellious young punk-rocker in Australia has more in common culturally with her conservative grandmother than she does with a fellow punk-rocker from Japan. I hasten to add, though, that she probably wouldn't agree with my opinion and nor would her grandmother!

Given that there are many factors influencing our behaviour and communication, how then do we distinguish the *source* of a particular example of either? Although it is an interesting exercise to research this question, it is not important for our purposes in this book. We can, instead, safely assume that *culture is always a potential influence on every aspect of behaviour and communication.*

It is important to recognise diversity, because there is a widespread tendency to ignore or reduce this diversity when we look at other cultures.

To fail to acknowledge diversity is to 'stereotype', one of the approaches most damaging to successful intercultural understanding. Actually, there are two problems with stereotyping:

- It reduces diversity (absolutely everyone in that culture is the same); and
- It reduces complexity (this culture can be described with only this small set of characteristics).

Both concepts are false.

Even if we are opposed to it in principle, we all stereotype: it is a quick and efficient way of storing information. We all do it. Do you, for example, have a stereotype of librarians, or of accountants?

Only an idealist would push for the eradication of stereotyping. But I *would* argue for being aware of what we do when we stereotype — that is essential. Even more importantly, we shouldn't use our stereotypes as the only source of information. We should be aiming to *expand* our interpretations, trying to recognise the diversity and complexity of what we see.

Another natural tendency which can be damaging is 'generalisation'. This is how it works. Let's say we see a member of our own culture do something we regard as negative. We tend to explain their negative behaviour in terms of their individual shortcomings ('That guy is so arrogant') or their circumstances ('He must be under a lot of pressure'). However when we see somebody from another culture do something we regard as negative, we may attribute their behaviour to their culture (*'Those people* are so arrogant'). The behaviour of the individual becomes the behaviour of the group.

Another tendency, in some ways opposite to generalisation, is what we call 'discounting'. You've probably heard it before:

A: What do you think of Malutians?
B: Oh, I can't stand them. They're rude, arrogant, only interested in...
A: What about Eks? He's Malutian.
B: Oh, I really like Eks. But he's *different*.

We are dealing with powerful forces here. People tend to have a more positive image of their own cultures than they do of other cultures. (Here we need to remember the distinction between culture and lifestyle, because tribes may well admire aspects of another tribe's lifestyle — its food, music, and artefacts, say.)

When asked to describe themselves, people invariably say that their tribe is 'friendly'. Other cultures (with a few notable exceptions) are seen as being less friendly, or they don't have as good a sense of humour, or they are not as hardworking or intelligent.

This is the tricky part — feelings of cultural superiority. Perhaps it is a natural world-wide phenomenon. Not only the view that 'we' are friendlier and so on, but the idea that we are better, or cleverer, more intelligent, more polite, more caring, more sensitive, or more successful, and so on. Perhaps we feel that our tribe has achieved more, or has made more material progress, or we are more attractive or bigger or cleaner, or we feel that we have a long and rich tradition. There seem to be three patterns, in descending order of frequency:

1. The first attitude is one of unquestioned superiority. This feeling of superiority may be accompanied by a wide range of emotions — indifference to other cultures, feeling sorry for other cultures, having a rather patronising concern to 'help' them, through to outright dislike and contempt for them.

2. The second attitude is characterised by recognising the *principle* of cultural equality. Here there is a *desire* to reduce or eliminate any feeling of superiority, even if there is actually no informed recognition of the worth and validity of the other culture.

3. The third, and by far the least common, approach is one of genuine exploration, in which people seek to see the other culture from its own perspectives and not judge it by external values. Its internal logic, its validity, its strengths are slowly uncovered and genuine respect emerges.

Clearly, this last attitude is the most useful and constructive, but it may not be practical to go around intensively exploring cultures.

The second attitude has some merit; it is at least based on a reasonable principle. But there is a risk that the principle may not stand up to practice. In actual intercultural contacts, the principle may start to crumble:

● One American writer has said this about her tribe: 'Most Americans genuinely believe that everyone should be given equal opportunity. But they baulk, in confusion, disillusionment, and dismay, when culturally different people fail to behave in expected (and they think self-evidently appropriate) ways.'[7]

Soon people find themselves saying things like 'well, I'm not racist, *but...*'. In other words: I want to cope with this, but I can't.

The first attitude, on the other hand, is going nowhere: it doesn't even have the desire to understand. It is based on ignorance and fear of differentness and relies on one's own standards to judge others.

Too often it goes like this. Imagine that you and your tribe are very familiar with, say, badminton and then you see a tennis match for the first time. You think they are trying to play badminton and you therefore judge their performance as unsuccessful and inferior — they're not serving correctly, they're using unsuitable equipment, they're not using the right strokes, and so on. You don't realise that they're not trying to play *your* game: they have their own!

Perhaps there is another way forward, somewhere between the second and third attitudes, without having to become full-time cultural explorers, and without having to rely on a well-intentioned principle that may fall apart under pressure. The approach goes something like this:

- This culture is successful in its own terms. It may not measure up to my own standards, but it works for them. I'll take whatever opportunities there are to learn more about their culture.

At the same time, it may also be important to recognise that a particular culture may be under enormous stress, either because of an internal problem (massive crime and drug problems, or economic problems, for example) or because of external reasons (suppression or exploitation by a more dominant culture). In these cases, I try to remember that all cultures, including my own, have had difficulties at different times in the past, or might have crises in the future. Again, the culture needn't be condemned.

I have visited and lived in quite a few cultures. I can honestly say that in *every* culture I have found things that I have admired and that have given me a new insight into the world — whether it is an aspect of social organisation, or how people interact, or how children are raised, or how problems are solved.

Equally, every culture (including my own) has things which have baffled or irritated me, or to which I have felt there is a 'better' approach possible. But instead of moving straight to condemnation, I have assumed that there must be a good reason (at least in their terms) for that behaviour. I don't have to understand it, I don't even have to like it. But I won't dismiss it. *And* I will quickly remind myself that there are aspects of my own tribe's behaviour which must baffle and irritate *them*. This approach doesn't always make the confusion or irritation disappear immediately, but it does help. Some people seem willing to condemn a whole culture because of what they perceive to be a few negative features — whereas, when pressed, they are quite willing to recognise negative features in their *own* culture — and yet *not* condemn it in its entirety.

Can you think of aspects of your culture that might baffle or irritate people from other cultures? As I was writing this, my mother and aunt happened to be visiting and I asked them this question. Their answers were interesting. After some consideration, they felt that our behaviour and attitudes might be seen by other cultures as self-interested and uncaring. What about *your* culture?

When talking of culture the concepts 'better' or 'worse' ultimately break down. By whose standards? The concept 'different' is safer and more reasonable.

🛇 Some cultures are better than others.

🛇 Cultural worth is in the eye of the beholder.

NO CULTURE IS AN ISLAND

Another widespread tendency is to fail to recognise the debt cultures owe each other, except to deplore those influences which are seen to be harmful. Cultures are not isolated: tribes have always been influenced by and borrowed from other tribes. At least some of the members of the tribe have made it through to (or 'traders' have come in from) regional and international 'marketplaces', bringing back new goods, new ideas, new beliefs (and often the new words to go with these novelties). While some of the imports have been at a more superficial 'lifestyle' level, others have had a profound effect.

Consider the following:

● What are the predominant religions in your tribe? How come?

● If you said 'yes' to any of the attitudinal changes listed on page 13 (attitudes towards marriage, women becoming engineers; smoking; young people choosing their marriage partners, etc) were these changes influenced by external sources or were they entirely internal?

One general caution needs to be expressed about cultural 'imports', however. Often when the imports are added to the existing cultural stock of a tribe, they are adapted and 'localised' and may not retain the same meaning or value as in the source culture. So, when the two cultures come together, they recognise similarity and fail to notice difference. Their *form* can be the same, but often their 'distribution' in the society (the situations in which they are used) can vary, and hence their meaning or significance. This can lead to misunderstanding and miscommunication.

Take the following examples, some of which are from language, some from culture.

● The word 'partner' has been adopted into urban Thai. Its 'form' is basically the same as in English, but its distribution (and therefore its meaning) is restricted to young women in places of entertainment with whom one dances for an hourly fee.

● Bicycles in Hong Kong and in China have the same form. Their distribution (and hence 'meaning') are, however, quite different. In the former, bicycles are means of recreation (and very seldom means of transport), while in China the reverse is true.

- The term/concept 'professor' has a different distribution and meaning in the United States compared with Australia.

This general pattern of difference in meaning and distribution applies even without any cultural importing. Tribes will *use the same resources differently* and ascribe different values to them. Again, a few examples:

- Speakers of English restrict the 'ng' sound to the ends of syllables ('si*ng*-er') and the ends of words ('thi*ng*'). When they confront languages which allow the sound at the beginning of words (for example, '*ng*ahm' in Thai), they may have difficulty, not because of the difference in form, but rather the difference in distribution.

- Different cultures ascribe different values to colours. In Australia, for example, 'yellow' and 'red' are associated with cowardice and anger respectively, while in China they are associated with pornography and prosperity. What do they 'mean' in your tribe?

- Thongs (flip-flops) are used in, among other places, both Australia and Indonesia, neighbouring cultures. The thongs have basically the same form in both tribes, but their distribution differs very significantly. Although there are some constraints on their distribution in Australia, these are not as strict as in Indonesia, where they are generally restricted to use at home. When Indonesians see Australians wearing thongs in public, this strikes them as strange and inappropriate behaviour.

- ✘ If something exists in two cultures, it is probably the same thing.
- ✍ Although two cultures may share the same item, its meaning and significance may not be the same.
- ✍ Don't assume that when you see something familiar in another culture that it has the same meaning and significance as in your own culture.

- Still on the issue of different meanings for the same object, I once sent a letter to an American friend living in Thailand, in which I enclosed a frangipani (plumeria) blossom. In my tribe, the distribution of this flower is unrestricted. The Thai women who saw my friend open the letter (and reveal the flower) were horrified as to my meaning and intention. In Thailand the frangipani tree is commonly grown in cemeteries and is therefore associated with death.

The flower anecdote may be trivial, but the differences in form, meaning, and distribution of shared human phenomena are of course fundamental and wide-reaching.

ACTION LIST

- Know what culture(s) you belong to.

- Understand that culture is pervasive. It influences the way you act, see, feel, do, interact, and behave.

- Accept that quite a lot of your own behaviour is rule-governed and ritualised. You are a member of a culture which regulates your behaviour.

- Don't make assumptions about other people's culture based on their ethnicity or nationality.

- Don't draw conclusions about a person's culture based on some aspect of their lifestyle.

- Don't assume that when you see something familiar in another culture that it has the same meaning and significance as in your own culture.

- Accept cultural difference as a reality. Underneath, the people of the world can be profoundly different.

- Don't make the mistake of thinking that your culture is more complex than others.

- Allow yourself to like and dislike aspects of other cultures, but don't condemn entire cultures.

- Remember that when you judge another culture you are probably using your own culture's standards to do so.

- Don't make the mistake of thinking that the people in your culture are diverse individuals, whereas the people in other cultures are indistinguishable.

- Accept that, although goodwill and tolerance provide a reasonable start, they are not enough. Look for the knowledge, awareness and skill needed to improve intercultural communication.

- Don't feel that you have to change your culture.

- Remember that your aim is to become a more skilled communicator, not a 'better' person.

- Remember that people have always succeeded in intercultural communication and always will.

- Try to avoid 'discounting' ('I don't like those people, but I like Eks. He's different.') If you are reacting positively to one person from that culture, there will be many other people in that culture you will relate to. He or she is not necessarily 'different'.

🍋 If you meet someone from another culture whom you don't like, don't generalise. Remember that this happens in your own culture (and you don't generalise and dismiss all of the people in your own culture).

🍋 Don't automatically assume that a person's negative behaviour is due to and typical of their culture. ('They're all like that.') That person's behaviour may be due to personality or to particular circumstances.

🍋 Accept that stereotyping is inevitable, but be aware that you are doing it, try to diminish it if possible, and don't use it as the only basis for your attitudes and interpretations.

And, finally, be realistic. Realise that, like all interpersonal matters, intercultural communication can be enjoyable, frustrating, puzzling, rewarding, irritating, fruitful, difficult, and fascinating.

Keeping the 'proper' distance

Different bodies, different hearts, different minds
Seeing differences across cultures

2

W HY worry about cultural difference? Surely if we just focus on the *similarities* across cultures, we'll be able to interact more successfully.

I wish it were that simple. Yes, there are tremendous similarities across cultures, and it is interesting to discover them. But it is the differences that prevail: this is the reality.

> The results of treating members of other cultures as though we are all programmed in the same way can range from the humorous through the painful to the tragic and even destructive. (Hall, 1984, p.6)

We don't have to learn all the *details* of these differences: that would be impossible, and unnecessary. But we do have to understand — really feel — what an impact culture can have and how different the tribes of the world can be.

Only by appreciating the depth and extent of cultural difference can we move forward. But where do we begin? After all, the list of differences is potentially so vast. In fact, the biggest collection in the world of research material on cultures,[1] which has data on over 300 cultures, investigates these cultures under 79 categories! They include things like Socialisation, Property, Law, Sex, Education, Marriage, Entertainment, and Sickness, and each of these sections in turn has between five and nine sub-categories! Socialisation, for example, has the following: techniques of inculcation, weaning and food training, cleanliness training, sex training, aggression training, independence training, transmission of cultural norms, transmission of skills, and transmission of beliefs.

We can't explore anything like that number, so let's tackle the issue in three broad categories: how does culture influence the body, the heart, and the mind?

CULTURE AND YOUR BODY
Can culture influence your body? We all have pretty much the same physiology, right? So, would you say, for example, that there are the same number of left-handers in different cultures? Consider your answer before looking at the research details below.

- 'Humans in the past 10,000 years, as well as now, have exhibited similar levels of left-handedness, usually involving less than 15 percent of the population. In those cultures where socialisation is lenient — such as the Eskimo, the boat people in Hong Kong, or the Australian aborigines — relatively high levels of left-handedness are seen. In those cultures where socialisation is severe, as among the Nigerians, the Hakka of Hong Kong, or the Temne, the percentage of left-handed persons is very low, reaching almost zero in the case of lower social class Nigerians. So, here is a nice example of the interaction between biology and culture. Biology fixes the range, and culture fixes the point within the range, at which behaviour takes place.'[2]

Culture limits what you can do with your left hand. If you are having difficulty in accepting this, try to think of a physical limit your culture places on you. Perhaps there is some aspect of eating or eye contact or sitting where your culture tells you what you can and *can't* do with your body.

Culture can actually alter your body, not just by imposing limits. Take, for example, the onset of puberty. Here is another arena where culture appears to impinge on physiology. Young women in all cultures go through puberty. At what age does this occur? Again, consider your answer before you look at some of the research findings. Can the differences be explained purely in physical terms — different genetic structure, different nutrition, for example? Or have collective attitudes (culture) had an impact?

- The age of puberty has fallen from 17 in Norway in 1850 to 13.5 in 1950 (with significant drops in Finland, Sweden, Denmark, USA also noted). The following differences were also noted in the same research study: three towns in Rumania 13.5; three village areas in Rumania 14.6; African Cubans 12.3; two highland peoples of Papua New Guinea 18.8 and 17.5.[3]

Alright, can culture influence your voice? Given that all tribes have the same voice-production 'equipment', will voices be the same across all tribes? Here is one research finding, which appears to illustrate that a cultural change has brought about a change in voices:

- 'Young women in Australia today have a lower fundamental note compared to voices of women 45 to 50 years. The increasingly masculine tone of the female voice is ascribed to social factors and the rise of the feminist movement.'[4]

Moving from the voice to the eyes, is the incidence of colour blindness the same in all cultures?

- 'Colour blindness in males is lowest in hunters/gatherers (Eskimos, Fijians, Navaho) and highest in groups farthest removed in time or habitat from hunters/gatherers (Arabs, Bombay Indians, Europeans, North American Whites, Japanese, etc.).'[5]

Here, finally, is one for parents! At what age should you start to train a child in bladder and bowel control and by what age will this usually be achieved? Do you have your answer ready? If so, now compare it to one tribe (the Digo people of Kenya) who initiate training at 2-3 weeks and expect that full bladder and bowel control will be achieved by the age of 5-6 months.[6]

Culture pushes, pulls, and inclines our bodies in ways that are 'acceptable'. Bow, stand straight, shake hands, raise your hands, rub noses, lift your plate to your mouth, don't lift your plate to your mouth, sit with your legs crossed, don't cross your legs, and so on. No matter how much we might think these are individual decisions, they are not — they are the decisions of the tribe (which we conform to or, of course, reject — and accept the consequences).

- Recently I was teaching a group of adult students in Hong Kong. Before the first class, I came early to the room, so that I could rearrange the furniture. The room had a large boardroom-style table which was modular, consisting of four sections. I carefully separated the sections, placing chairs around each isolated section. I did this for two reasons: I prefer small-group work in a class, and also I calculated that it was impossible for the twenty-two of us to fit around the table. When the students entered, they were clearly puzzled and disoriented by this arrangement. The following week, the students arrived before me (deliberately?) and were happily sitting around the reunited table, chairs jammed together and shoulders touching (or with no more than a one-inch gap). I asked whether they were comfortable. They collectively smiled and declared they liked it this way, and the class proceeded, in a very relaxed manner.

In recent decades an enormously rich field of study has developed which examines how we use the space between us and other people and things around us, and how this varies from culture to culture.

Researchers find, for example, significant differences cross-culturally in the distance that people stand from each other when they talk. It has been shown that when Americans are talking with a casual acquaintance, they stand at almost twice the distance that Arabs use in a similar situation.[7] Have you found a difference in preferred distance in communicating with people from other cultures?

Here are a number of other instances[8] of mis-match on issues of managing space, again exemplified with Arabs and Americans :

- 'An Arab friend seemed unable to walk and talk at the same time. After years in the United States, he could not bring himself to stroll along, facing forward while talking. Our progress would be arrested while he edged ahead, cutting slightly in front of me and turning sideways so we could see each other. Once in this position, he would stop. His behaviour was explained when I learned that for the Arabs to view the other person

25

peripherally is regarded as impolite. You must be involved when interacting with Arabs who are friends.'

- Another Arab subject remarked, referring to American behaviour (the physical distance they maintained in conversation), 'What's the matter? Do I smell bad? Or are they afraid of me?'

- 'An elderly Arab diplomat in an American hospital felt that his nurse "didn't care" and was ignoring him, because the nurse was using appropriate (for American) "professional distance".'

- 'Another Arab informant said that he was in constant hot water with Americans because of the way he looked at them without the slightest intention of offending. Arabs look each other in the eye when talking with an intensity that makes most Americans highly uncomfortable'.

Here is a sample of reported instances[9] (this time taken from four cultures) of people interacting with their spatial environments and with each other. Are there similarities with your culture?

- 'It is rude for a guest to walk around the Arab home eyeing things.'

- 'Arabs don't mind being crowded by people but hate to be hemmed in by walls.'

- 'The study of Japanese gardens illustrates their habit of leading the individual to a spot where he can discover something for himself.'

- 'There is no Japanese word for "privacy".'

- 'No matter where one sits to contemplate the scene (in a Japanese garden), one of the rocks that make up the garden is always hidden.'

- 'Traditionally, the Japanese name intersections rather than the streets leading into them.'

- 'The Japanese have been known to say that our (American) rooms look bare, because the centres are bare (with much of the furniture being arranged around the walls).'

- 'In offices, Americans keep doors open; Germans keep doors closed. In Germany, the closed door does not mean that the man behind it wants to be alone or undisturbed, or that he is doing something he doesn't want someone else to see. It's simply that Germans think that open doors are sloppy and disorderly.'

- 'A German newspaper editor who had moved to the United States had his visitor's chair bolted to the floor "at the proper distance" because he couldn't tolerate the American habit of adjusting the chair to the situation.'

Virtually all aspects of our physical interaction with people and with our environments will be influenced by culture, that set of unconscious group decisions about behaviour.

How do you handle the following 'spatial situations' in your tribe? Squeezing past people to get a seat in a cinema or theatre, which way do you face? Can you step over? Standing in a crowded lift, do you look at each other or carefully divert your eyes (up, down, or away)? When passing something to someone, how do you indicate politeness or respect? If you need to walk between two people who are talking, do you walk straight, dip, or say anything?

- People in all cultures manage their bodies in pretty much the same way.
- Cultures have profoundly different rules governing their bodies.
- When in an intercultural situation, observe how people manage their bodies.

OBSERVATION CHECKLIST

The following list is only a small sample of the kind of things you could observe in your own culture and in other cultures. These areas are likely to contain cultural difference:

- sitting
- passing things
- greeting each other
- holding hands (who can; who can't?)
- walking past people (what do you do?)
- walking through the door (who's first?)

- standing
- touching each other
- placement of hands
- ways of eating (what's polite; what's not?)
- sneezing, belching, spitting (what's OK, what's not?)
- managing the body (what's good; what's not?)

CULTURE AND YOUR MIND

Now let's look at this whole business of 'the mind' logically. After all, logic is logic, right? Unchangeable, objective and universal. Well, no. Logic seems to be as subjective and as culture-specific as anything else. In fact, one of the pioneers of research into cultural difference claims that: 'There must be hundreds of different systems of logic in the world.'

To test this out, let's just take one small example. 'The future lies ahead of us and the past behind us.' Is that correct? Is it logical? OK, now try to disprove it and establish that the opposite is in fact logical. If you give up, read on.

- Some cultures in Papua New Guinea would argue that since we cannot 'see' the future, then, logically, it must be behind us. We can, on the other hand 'see' the past. It must, logically, therefore lie in front of us, i.e. in our field of vision.[10]

Now, which concept is correct: is the future behind us or in front of us? Clearly, there is no 'correct', no 'better'.

- Don't assume your way is *the* way.
- Be ready for different approaches.
- See that other ways are valid.
- Try to avoid 'good', 'bad', 'better', 'right' cross-culturally.

Let's try another dimension, again a possible candidate for great similarity across cultures: the concept of time. Look at the following statement:

- 'Oh, my goodness! I was having such a good time. I had no idea it was getting so late. Boy, time flies when you're having a good time.'

Try translating this statement into other languages that you know (or ask someone to do so, if you have access to bilingual people). Is there any difficulty in carrying out the translation? Check the translation — does it actually use the equivalent word for 'time' in the expressions 'having a good time' and 'time flies'. How is the idea of 'getting late' expressed? Does the translation seem natural to a monolingual speaker of that language? (Remember that bilingual speakers sometimes allow one language to influence the other!)

If you do encounter difficulty, or if concepts are conveyed very differently, this would hardly be surprising. Research shows very considerable difference in the way tribes conceptualise time. Actually, the differences begin even with how we *measure* time, as the following two examples illustrate.

We need to have a system for organising and numbering the 24 hours in a day. For example:

1 2 3 4 5 6 7 8 9 10 11 12 (a.m.)
1 2 3 4 5 6 7 8 9 10 11 12 (p.m.)

Are there any other ways to organise and number the 24 hours in a day (apart from the 1–24 system used frequently in such contexts as transport)? The people of Thailand, for example, organise it as follows:

1 2 3 4 5 6
1 2 3 4 5 6
1 2 3 4 5 6
1 2 3 4 5 6

Let's take another concrete example. In some dialects of English, a speaker may refer to 'half seven'. A speaker of Dutch can, coincidentally, use the same two words, 'half seven' (with slightly different pronunciation). Are they referring to the same time? What are the two possible meanings? (7.30 in the former case, and 6.30 in the latter.)

The diversity is even greater when it comes to *concepts* of time. Let's return to our English speaker, again trying to translate (or get translations of) the statements you read.

- 'Time is money.'
- 'You're wasting my time.'
- 'This gadget will save you hours.'
- 'I don't have the time to give you.'
- 'How do you spend your time these days?'
- 'That flat tire cost me an hour.'
- 'I've invested a lot of time in her.'
- 'I don't have enough time to spare for that.'
- 'You're running out of time.'
- 'You need to budget your time.'
- 'Put aside some time for ping pong.'
- 'Is that worth your while?'
- 'Do you have much time left?'
- 'He's living on borrowed time.'
- 'You don't use your time profitably.'
- 'I lost a lot of time when I got sick.'
- 'Thank you for your time.'[11]

Clearly, in this tribe time is seen as an asset, something you can have, put aside, or lose. It is a valuable *commodity*. How did your translation go?

Of course *anything* in one language (culture) can be translated into another language (culture), so that the person at least understands it, even if he doesn't *feel* it in the same way as the original speaker. (When people claim that a certain word or expression in their native language is untranslatable, they are both right and wrong, depending on the level of translatability you are seeking.)

Does your language have tenses (as in English, for example: She *plays* tennis. She *played* tennis yesterday.)? English — and quite a few other languages — treat time as a line divided into past, present, and future. As one linguist put it, 'somehow we have managed to objectify or externalise our imagery of the passage of time, which makes it possible for us to feel that we can manage time, control it, spend it, save it, or waste it. We have a feeling that the process of "becoming later" is real and tangible, because we can attach a numerical value to it.'[12] He goes on to compare this approach to the American Indian language Hopi.

- 'The Hopi language does not do this. No past, present, or future exists as verb tenses in their language. Hopi verbs have no tenses. In English

29

and other European languages, temporal terms such as summer and winter are nouns, which gives them a material quality because they can be treated like any other noun, numbered and given plurals. In other words, they are treated as objects. The Hopi seasons are treated more like adverbs... The Hopi cannot talk about summer being hot, because summer is the quality hot, just as an apple has the quality red. Summer and hot are the same. There is nothing about summer that suggests it involves time... in the sense that is conveyed by English and other European languages.'[13]

✘ Some languages can't distinguish between the present and the past.

✘ My language is more precise than yours.

✎ All languages can, in their own way, distinguish between present and past events, but they may not feel that this distinction is important enough to create a system of verb tense.

✎ If a language does not do something that your language does, don't think of that language (and its speakers) as being deficient in some way. It simply has other priorities. There are bound to be things in that language which your language 'can't do'.

Time gets us into all sorts of problems interculturally. To take just one example, English speakers often react negatively to being told, by speakers of Spanish, that something will be ready by '*mañana*' (tomorrow) and then finding that it is not actually ready the next day. Accusations of dishonesty or unreliability start flying. Yet these same speakers would be astonished if they got a similar response to their saying 'I'll be ready in a minute' or 'I'll be there in a second' — or that someone took them literally when they say 'We really must get together some time'!

To return to our analysis of time, one scholar claims that societies organise time in at least two different ways:

1. 'monochronic time', where events are seen as separate items — one thing at a time — with greater emphasis on the management of sequencing and the value of events; or

2. 'polychronic time', where people may be involved in several things at once, with greater emphasis on fluidity, and greater value on people rather than events, so that scheduling may be sacrificed to maintaining good relations.

Two examples are provided: 'The Japanese are polychronic when looking and working inward, toward themselves. When dealing with the outside world, they have adopted monochronic time. The French are monochronic intellectually but polychronic in behaviour.'[14] Which of these two descriptions comes closer to your own tribe's use of and concept of time?

By the way, before we leave the issue of time. Are we living in the twentieth century? Before you leap to answer, you should note that it is the twenty-sixth century in Thailand, and the fifteenth century in Saudi Arabia, to take just two different measures of the passage of time.

✖ Some things, such as time, are universal.

∅ Few things, even time, are universal.

∅ Your concept of time is not *the* concept of time.

∅ Observe people's concepts of time and attitudes towards time in other cultures.

OBSERVATION CHECKLIST

The following list is only a small sample of the kind of things you might observe about 'time' in your own culture and in other cultures.

- What are the attitudes towards time, as exemplified by punctuality?
- Is there an emphasis on the separation of events in time, as exemplified by the importance of schedules?
- Do people 'get down to business' or do they work on their relationship first?

Time to move on, this time to the issue of language. Here few people will need convincing that there are substantial differences from tribe to tribe. But in what ways do languages differ?

Too often people assume that languages differ only in the different words for things, so that translation involves finding the equivalent word and putting it in that slot. If only it were that simple!

We've seen above how a certain concept (that of 'time') will influence, and be reflected in a language. Here now are other ways of examining languages and their diversity.

Let's begin with the issue of sequence. English usually places its subjects, verbs and objects in that order. For example: *Children* (S) *like* (V) *toys* (O).

What other sequences are possible and might occur in other languages? There are of course six possible sequences, including the SVO pattern of English, and — yes — all six combinations can be found in the world's languages.

Children like toys.
Children toys like.
Like children toys.
Like toys children.
Toys children like.
Toys like children.

Guess which pattern is the most common among the world's languages? The most common sequence is SOV (*Children toys like*). Which pattern is correct? Of course, none of them is universally, objectively 'correct'. Different groups of people have over a period of time 'decided' on one particular pattern, making it correct for *them*.

We saw above that English puts information about time on to every verb it uses (in the form of tense). What other information do you think could be put on to verbs when people communicate?

After you have considered the possibilities, read a few 'answers' below. We can begin to see how values and perceptions are coded into the language, reinforcing (in every act of communication every day) those same values and perceptions — or perhaps it is the other way round. It is largely this that people are referring to when they quite rightly say that language and culture are inseparable.

- 'The Hopi people indicate the validity of a statement, that is, the nature of the relationship between the speaker and his knowledge or experience of that about which he is speaking. When a Hopi says, "It rained last night," the hearer knows how that Hopi speaker knew it rained: whether he was out in the rain and got wet; looked outside and saw it raining; whether someone came through the door and said it was raining; or he woke up in the morning and saw that the ground was wet and assumed that it had rained.'[15] Note that the English speaker only gets information about the time of the event: it happened in the past (which is redundant anyway in this example, given the time expression.) The information that the Hopi verb conveys could of course be conveyed in English, but it has not been coded in 'shorthand' on to the English verb.

- The Thai people give information about the status of the person being spoken to or spoken about. They do this (among many other ways) by completely changing the verb itself. Thus, entirely different words will be used to convey 'eating' if it is being done by a high-status person, a medium-status person, a low-status person, a monk, or a member of the royal family. Neither the validity of or the source of the speaker's knowledge of the event, nor the time it occurred, are coded on to the verb.

What about nouns: the objects and entities in our world that we constantly refer to in our communication? What information do English speakers automatically code on to their nouns? We must give information about *number* (singular/plural) and occasionally we give information about *gender* ('actor/actress'). But there are many other possibilities, including: What *shape* is it? What *type* of thing is it?

Let us now look at pronouns, where the diversity is, not surprisingly, very great; this is after all how we call and refer to each other. If your language has only one word to refer to yourself ('*I*') and one to refer to the person you're talking to ('*you*'), what variations do you think other languages might have? In other words, what information do languages code into their pronouns? Consider the possibilities before you read on:

- Languages often make distinctions of gender, status, and intimacy/distance in their pronouns. The Thai language has all three: women and men refer differently to themselves ('I') and both choose from a range of about twelve alternatives to express their relative status and intimacy with the person they're talking to ('you'). When referring to a third person or persons ('he/she/they'), status distinctions are possible, but there is no reference to gender or to number. If you like, there is basically one word that is equivalent to the English 'he/she/they'. The overall system is, however, still more complex than this. Instead of using any of the above pronouns, Thais will often use nouns indicating their relationship to somebody. ('Younger person brought older person some fruit' = 'I brought you some fruit'). Yet another system is to use personal names only. ('Lek brought Noi some fruit' = 'I brought you some fruit'). If your language is English and you are feeling that this Thai system is (unnecessarily) complex, you might like to explain to a Thai person the need to distinguish between the following alternatives: 'She plays tennis, she is playing tennis, she has played tennis, she has been playing tennis, she had been playing tennis, she would have played tennis, she is going to play tennis, she will be playing tennis' and so on.

- My language is more polite than yours, because I can choose between a wide selection of words for 'you' to express my respect and deference to another person.

- All languages can, in their own way, make fine distinctions of respect and deference to other people, but they may not choose to do this with their choice of pronouns.

Our emotional relationship to our languages is very tight. We tie the word and the thing that it refers to into one indivisible entity, so that, for example, an 'apple' is an apple. This tight linkage may be particularly true for monolingual people, who have not had to assign another word, say the Russian *yabloka*, to that thing. This bonding of the thing and the name can be quite strong. I have seen speakers of English take up *yabloka* (for 'apple') easily enough, but have greater difficulty in referring to *Bog* (the Russian word for 'God').

It is impossible to separate language from culture, particularly its perceptions and values. We have seen this illustrated with concepts of time (above), but it of course applies much more broadly. Again taking English as an example, we see how argumentation tends to be conceptualised as 'war', something to be won or lost. Consider the following examples: 'Your claims are indefensible'; 'He attacked every weak point in my argument'; 'His criticisms were right on target'; 'I demolished his argument'; 'He shot down all my arguments'.[16] This concept (or metaphor, if you prefer) is not universal.

The richness of language is inexhaustible. Before we leave the topic, try just a few more possibilities. I have not provided the answers to the following questions, but rather my aim is to sow the seed of doubt in your mind (that your normal system may not be universal):

- If your tribe uses only one concept/word for '*we*', what other possibilities can you imagine?
- Do all written languages use punctuation?
- English is written left-to-right, top-to-bottom. What other possibilities are there?
- In addressing an envelope, one system starts with the name of the addressee and ends with the name of the country. What other possibilities can you envisage?

Finally, a general point about *attitudes* towards language. Many people argue that one language is better than another, more descriptive, more poetic, more precise, more complex, or more expressive. These views are understandable, but it is important to note, however, that this is not a view shared by linguists. Two personal experiences come to mind on this issue:

- The first happened twenty years ago when I was doing a university assignment in which we had to analyse some data from one of the Australian Aboriginal languages. I was complaining, over a cup of coffee with student friends, about the difficulty of the task and the grammatical complexity of the languages in my assignment. My friends were astonished: surely these languages, spoken by people with a less sophisticated material society than their own, would not have a complex grammar. Then, and since then, I have been able to persuade very few people of the richness of Australian Aboriginal languages.
- The second experience was more recent. A teaching colleague announced quite unequivocally that Cantonese had no metaphors and that German was a 'descriptive' language. Neither claim, of course, has any substance.

Granted, we may have personal preferences regarding the 'beauty' of a language (not a recognised linguistic concept, I must hasten to assure you), or we may admire some certain speakers or writers of a particular language, but our evaluations of languages can go no further. Claims for greater sophistication or precision or complexity are, frankly, nonsense. Linguists hold the view that all languages are highly complex and communicatively equivalent.

Some people may feel that there are languages (such as English, French, and Spanish) which, because they are widespread, must have some inherent qualities of superiority over other languages. This is certainly *not true*. These languages have become widespread because of political, economic and social circumstances. Other languages have in the past been pre-eminent (Latin, for example); still other languages may become more widespread in the future.

- ✗ Some languages are better than others.
- ✗ Some languages are more beautiful than others.
- ✗ Some languages are more sophisticated than others.
- ✓ All languages are successful.
- ✓ All languages are complex.
- ✓ Sophistication is a subjective concept which is 'in the eye of the beholder'.
- ✓ Reduce your linguistic chauvinism.
- ✓ Recognise the success and complexity of all languages.
- ✓ Realise that your language reflects and influences the way you see the world.
- ✓ Realise that other people's languages reflect and influence the way they see the world.

OBSERVATION CHECKLIST

The following list is only a small sample of the kind of things you might observe about language in your own culture and in other cultures.

- Look at the verbs to see what information they provide about the tribe's view of the world.
- Look at the nouns to see what information they provide about the tribe's view of the world.
- Look at the pronouns to see what information they provide about the tribe's view of themselves.

OK, let's stop talking and think… Surely, here, there must be considerable similarity across cultures. Well, there is, but there is also considerable difference. Cultures can look at the same thing and see it differently. We are trained/programmed by our experience, needs and our values to perceive our environments accordingly, resulting in differences across cultures. Here are just a few examples, illustrating the culture-specific nature of perception.

⚹ There are objective realities.

∅ Our perceptions are biased and subjective.

● The people of the Trobriand Islands can see a boy's resemblance to his father, but not to his brother or mother, even if this might be very apparent to an outsider. Researchers are convinced that they are not merely avoiding admitting such a (taboo) resemblance; *they actually cannot see it.*[17]

● On a more personal level, my physical appearance has been perceived in many different ways by the different tribes among whom I have lived. In some societies people have consistently guessed my age to be double the actual figure. When I have revealed my true age, the invariable response has been 'But you're so big!' (I am 187cm or 6'3" tall.) Similarly, my hair has been variously described as red, blonde, yellow, white, sandy, and brown. (I would probably say it's blonde, for whatever that perception is worth.)

The same appears to be true for memory. Influenced by different needs and value systems, research has shown that people from different cultures, having heard the same narration, will remember quite different details. The results are quite consistent within each cultural group, showing the *group* basis to perception and thinking. The way we think and see appears to be more than just an individual effort. In even highly individualistic tribes, social pressure can alter both.

● In experiments where collaborators were instructed to lie about what they saw, uninformed members of the group agreed with their lies. Before you leap to declare your individuality and independence, you should note that similar results have been reported with American, Brazilian, Lebanese, Hong Kong Chinese and Fijian college students, and somewhat higher levels of conformity in Zimbabwean and Fijian Indian students. Close questioning of the students who took part in the American experiments suggested that the desire to conform did not just lead them to lie about what they saw: *it actually caused them to see what the others said they saw.*[18]

∅ The perceptions of the individual relate to the perceptions of the group.

What about the way we think — the way, for example, we solve problems? Again, there are differences. One analysis shows two broad approaches to problem-solving: a 'generalised problem-solving orientation' where there is emphasis on applying awareness and experience gained from previous problem-solving to any new problem. The other is a 'particularistic' orientation, where specific solutions are sought to each new problem.

Similarly, there are broadly at least two styles of analysis — either focusing on the details (an analytical style) or seeing the whole picture (a global style).

When it comes to learning, again there are many different styles, including learning from observation of a correct model, learning through explicit instruction, and learning by pooling group knowledge and experience, to name just three.

Needless to say, these differences have implications for various kinds of tests used for educational or employment purposes. You may have read criticisms of IQ tests or various kinds of entrance tests for being culturally biased. (Many American commentators, for example, have felt that Afro-American students are disadvantaged by tests that are specific to Anglo-American ways of seeing and learning.)

- 'One spectacular failure was reported by the author of the Porteus Maze tests, which he believed to be culture-free. When he administered them to Australian Aboriginals, he found it difficult to persuade his subjects to solve the problems by their own efforts. Used to arriving at decisions after discussing them with others until a solution had been reached, they were very much surprised that Porteus would not help them, especially in the case of one tribe which had just made him an "honorary member".'[19]

The quest for a culture-free test appears to be still elusive, an important point that should be remembered by administrators and users of standardised 'intelligence' and 'aptitude' tests.

OBSERVATION CHECKLIST

The following list is only a small sample of the kind of things you might observe in your own culture and in other cultures:

- What levels of society (classes, etc.) does the tribe seem to recognise? What are these based on?
- Who seems to get the respect of other people in the tribe?
- What is the status of teachers in the tribe?
- What kind of teaching and learning methods are used in schools?
- How do parents and children interact?
- How do parents 'socialise' their children? How is discipline exercised?

CULTURE AND YOUR HEART

I have chosen to describe issues of emotion and attitudinal judgements (likes and dislikes, preferences) as being centred in the *heart*. This concept, although widespread among cultures, is not universal. Tribes may regard the stomach, the head, or indeed other parts of the body, as being the seat of emotion.

Regardless of where they might be located, aren't emotions the same everywhere? Certainly there does seem to be a core set of emotions that all peoples share, and 'each of the basic human emotions (such as happiness, sadness, fear, anger, surprise) seem to be associated with the same distinctive movements of the facial muscles in a wide variety of cultures'.[20] *But* ... two words of caution. 'The rules for controlling facial behaviour vary across cultures'. Also, emotional expressions may have different meanings and different distributions. Laughter, to take just one example, does not have the same meaning in all cultures.

- I vividly remember seeing a Thai driver accidentally bump his car into the rear of another car, driven by an American. When both drivers got out of the cars and surveyed the damage, the Thai person began to laugh. The American (assuming only one function for laughter) became angry, which in turn led to even more smiling and laughter from the Thai man. Clearly, there are other meanings to laughter beside amusement; in this case, it was a (culturally appropriate) expression of embarrassment and discomfort. Another case of form, distribution, and meaning.

Similarly, emotions are not necessarily present to the same extent in the same situations.

- In comparing children's responses to the same anxiety-provoking situations, researchers found that Hungarian and Japanese children exhibited greater anxiety than Swedish children. (In the two European cultures, incidentally, girls showed greater anxiety than boys, but in Japan there were no differences according to sex.)[21]

Same emotional equipment, different forms, distribution, and meanings.

OBSERVATION CHECKLIST
The following list is only a small sample of the kind of things you might observe in your own culture and in other cultures.

- What function does laughter have? Does it have more than one meaning?
- What limits seem to be imposed on the expression of emotion? Do these limits apply equally to everyone?
- Which is preferred — honestly expressing your emotions, whether positive or negative, or controlling them?

Let's go even deeper, and consider the issue of self-identification — how you see yourself.

To test how you see yourself, look at the following list. Each item in the list presents a characteristic which people may use to identify themselves. Which characteristics do you use to identify yourself?

- gender
- ethnicity
- occupation or profession
- pursuit or pastime
- family role (father, son, daughter, mother, etc.)
- religion
- tribe/culture
- nation
- education
- age
- sexuality
- area of residence
- region of birth

Clearly, we do not have one fixed identity. It will depend on the circumstances of a particular context. I may choose certain memberships to define myself when I am acting as a lecturer with a group of university students (my age-group, for example, my education, and of course my profession) and quite a different set when chatting to a person in an airport lounge (perhaps my nationality, my ethnicity, or my pastimes), and yet another set when I am with my uncle. Which characteristics do you think might come to the fore in a context of intercultural contact?

Here are some other ways of testing your self-identity. As you are becoming acquainted with someone (at a party, say, or at work) how do you present yourself to that person? Of the categories of information listed above that are not immediately apparent to the other person, which would you present, and in what order? Similarly, what do you tend to find out about the other person? Do these concerns carry over into life decisions, for example, into choosing a marriage partner? What would you hope for in marriage partners for your children? With whom do you usually maintain social contact?

This leads us to the critical issue of socialisation and social organisation. Clearly, this is an enormous area, so we will look briefly only at a small cross-section of features and examples.

The first example looks at child-raising methods and comes from a landmark research study called the Six Cultures Project:[22]

- In this project children's behaviour towards their mothers was compared, with two 'dimensions' of behaviour emerging as critical:

  (a) did the children tend to be 'dependent' (asking for resources from their mother) or 'responsible' (offering her resources); and

  (b) were they 'sociable' (expressing warmth towards their mother) or 'aggressive' (acting more distant from their mother).

In the six cultures surveyed, four patterns emerged:

1. responsible and sociable: Juxtlahuaca (Mexico) and Tarong (Philippines)
2. dependent and aggressive: Khalapur (India) and Taira (Japan)
3. responsible and aggressive: Nyansongo (Kenya)
4. dependent and sociable: Orchard Town (U.S.A.)

If you happen to be from one of these six tribes, don't try to deny the research results! The research study was carried out very carefully.

Apart from child-raising, the second most widely surveyed area of social behaviour has been to do with marriage. One of these surveys looked at post-marital residence patterns in 859 societies spread across six continents. What is the most common pattern in your tribe? Do newly married couples tend to live with the man's family, the woman's family, or apart from their families? What percentage of the societies surveyed would you estimate have as their normal pattern that newly married couples live apart from the relatives of both spouses after marriage? (Answer: Only 5% of the societies surveyed had this as their dominant pattern.)[23]

Let us consider the issue of social stratification. How does any particular society sort itself into sub-groups or levels of people? What criteria are used to distinguish these strata, and how strong are the distinctions made? A society with castes, for example, has quite marked stratification, while other societies may try to blur any distinctions, but might still recognise working class, middle class and upper class. Here again a survey has been conducted, this time of 818 societies, dividing them into three broad categories: (a) complex occupational and elite stratification present, (b) distinction based on present possession of property but not crystallised into distinct and hereditary social classes, (c) absence of significant class distinctions, although stratification by individual skill, valour, piety, or wisdom may be present. What percentage of the societies surveyed would you estimate are represented by the three categories? (Answer: The findings were: 32%, 20% and 48%, respectively.)[24]

What social stratification is there in your tribe? How are you able to see membership of a particular stratum (or 'class' if you prefer) of society: through language, accent, appearance, material wealth, some other features? Where do you lie in the social strata of your tribe? Does your tribe generally (i) mark these strata clearly and then work out ways of negotiating between them; or (ii) try to down-play stratification and negotiate as if they did not exist? What will happen if you move across cultures representing these two broad patterns?

Finally, how do people go about achieving things in their societies, within and across their social strata — for example, getting jobs, gaining services, or negotiating bureaucratic obstacles? Do people use their membership networks to gain advantage and ease their path? Before you answer 'no' (as perhaps some English-speaking tribes might be tempted to do), consider the following: What does the expression 'old boy network' refer to? Or suppose, in a bureaucratic setting, you have a choice of two counters to go to. The officials behind these two counters differ visibly in their relative co-membership with you (for example, in ethnicity, gender, age, perhaps religion). Which of the two would you go to?

Much has been written (often disparagingly and often by Westerners) about the use of connections in other societies, without recognising their own use of networks of connections. Having said this, it is indisputable that some tribes place particular emphasis on networks of influence. (If you would like to read more about the issue of networking in a culture, you might like to read the section on 'guanxi' in Jean Brick's cultural study, *China*.)

People less familiar with the use of a wide range of networks who find themselves suffering disadvantage or delay in a cultural setting which places a high value on networks might like to consider the following perspective.

- 'If (a person) has to wait, it simply indicates that either he is not connected, and therefore not worth bothering about, or he doesn't know how to get along with others and has no friends. Either of these is an indictment.'[25]

Finally, we will reserve our greatest attention in this chapter for the issue of *values*. Here is the real bedrock of culture, and perhaps the greatest source of difficulty in intercultural interactions.

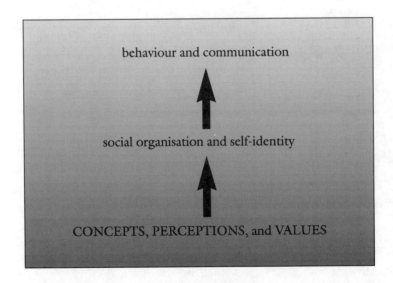

In one of the parables of the New Testament (Matthew 21:28–30) a man asks his two sons to do some work for him in the vineyard. One said he would not, but then relented and did the work; the second said he would, but didn't. Which behaviour, the first or the second son's, would you value more highly?

One writer on culture decided that the Westerner would give credit to the first son, while the Arabs would consider the second, who showed respect for his father although he did not follow through, more admirable.[26] At issue here is 'values'. One author has defined a 'value' as 'a broad tendency to prefer certain states of affairs over others'.[27]

Values underlie everything. Let's say, for example, that you are describing a person in your tribe. You decide that she lives in a 'nice' house, has a 'good' job, is a really 'good' mother, is a very 'kind' and 'friendly' person, has a 'good' sense of humour, is a 'terrific' hostess, a 'good' neighbour, a 'good' cook but a 'terrible' gardener. In general, she is a really 'good' person and she has really 'succeeded' in life. She's 'happy'. None of these judgements — 'good', 'nice', successful', and so on — make sense without some kind of *group* agreement. They are subjective judgements based on culture. They are judgements driven by the values system of the tribe. Needless to say, if a different tribe were to judge this woman using *their* value systems, the verdict may be quite different.

You can begin to examine your own cultural values, *your* preferences. From the list below, what do you regard as the five most important characteristics that you would look for in selecting an assistant at work, doing, say, a semi-clerical, semi-technical job in an architecture firm. Remember: your aim is to find the 'best' candidate.

self-confident	punctual	easily influenced
unemotional	independent	patient
reliable	thorough	industrious
emotional	takes risks	flexible
easygoing	cooperative	active
ambitious	can admit mistakes	takes initiative
serious	obedient	humble
aggressive	honest	pious
good sense of humour	passive	sexy
loyal	helpful	responsible
attractive	excitable	conservative
assertive	competitive	calm

Are there any characteristics that you would add to the list? Which five characteristics would you rank the lowest? If you have an opportunity, compare your answers with people from other cultures, especially those with little experience of your own culture. You may be astonished by their answers.

While your answer would naturally depend to some extent on the exact nature of the job and the company (and on your own individual preferences), there are nevertheless culture-specific patterns in the selections, both in this particular example, and more generally on the question of values.

- In a cross-cultural study of twenty values,[28] it was found that in parts of India status and glory were valued most, whereas courage, power, and wealth were not valued (the latter because of associations with arrogance and fear of thieves). The Greeks valued punishment (associated with justice) and power. The Japanese valued serenity and aesthetic satisfaction and disvalued ignorance, deviation and loneliness. What relative value do you think your tribe would give to these particular values?

- Another study[29] found that Indonesian high-school students attached greater importance to social responsibility than to individualism by contrast with Western students. Where do you think your tribe stands on this issue? Would there be a difference between the generations in your tribe (in other words, is your culture undergoing a change of values)?

- Yet another study,[30] this time of students in Papua New Guinea and Australia, found that the former ranked social recognition as a more important value than self-respect and placed obedience above independence, while Australian students ordered both pairs of values in the opposite direction. How do you think students in your tribe would compare?

- In comparing the cultures of North America and Mexico, one author had this to say: 'Where a Mexican will talk about a person's inner qualities in terms of the person's soul or spirit (*alma* or *espiritu*), North Americans are likely to feel uncomfortable using such words to talk about people. They may regard such talk as vague or sentimental, the words seeming to describe something invisible and hence unknowable, or at the very least "too personal". The unwillingness to talk in this way only confirms the view held by many Mexicans that North Americans are insensitive.'[31] Does your tribe commonly refer to a person's spirit or soul?

- In asking people in different cultures how they would define friendship, I have noticed that two key words appear sooner or later in people's descriptions. In some cultures the key word is 'share' and in others the key word seems to be 'support'. Which of these central concepts would you lean towards in defining friendship?

- In another major cross-cultural study,[32] the researchers found that Americans rated love and friendship as the most important life concerns and health as the 5th priority; Koreans ranked these 12th, 14th, and 19th respectively. What topped the Korean list? To be honest, I don't know: I don't have the full research results available. This surely is the point: when we encounter other cultures, we are in the dark about their value systems, and we need therefore to assume that we don't know their value systems.

Again, the tennis/badminton image we used above (p.17) is appropriate here.

✖ We all agree on the fundamentals of life.
✔ What's important to you is not necessarily important to another culture.
✔ People in other cultures are not necessarily trying to achieve the same things as you.
✔ Cultures may share the same values, but try to achieve them differently.

Values have been referred to as being 'among the building blocks of culture'.[33] They relate to an extremely wide range of critical aspects of our lives. What is a 'good' person? What is a 'friend'? What is 'love'? What is 'a successful marriage'? What is 'success'? — to name just a few.

Try this. Here are three interrelated parts of a value system. How would your tribe feel about them?

1. Apart from social and educational influences, people are basically the same;
2. Each person should be judged on his or her own individual merits;
3. These 'merits', including a person's worth and character, are revealed through the person's actions.

Do you accept this value system? If you do, remember that other tribes will reject it totally! Conversely, if you reject it, remember that other tribes believe this value system unquestioningly.

When different value systems come together, there can be problems, as the following illustrates: One of the pioneers of research into language and culture[34] examined bullfighting as an instance of 'cross-cultural misunderstanding'. Seen in Spanish culture as a sport which displays bravery and symbolises the triumph of art over the brute force of the bull, it is often regarded by American observers as the senseless slaughter of a defenceless animal in front of a cruel public.

Underlying these different attitudes there is a range of concepts and language features, which may help to explain the different attitudes of the two cultures to the same activity:

AMERICAN CULTURE/LANGUAGE	SPANISH CULTURE/LANGUAGE
Both animals and people have 'legs', 'necks' and 'backs.	There are distinct words for the 'legs', 'necks' and 'backs' of animals and people.
Animals get nervous.	Animals do not get nervous.
Animals have hospitals and cemeteries.	Animals do not have hospitals and cemeteries.
Man is physically strong.	Man is not physically strong, but is skilful and intelligent.
A bull has feelings of pain and sorrow.	A bull is strong, but not skilful and intelligent.

Is your tribe familiar with bullfighting? What do they think of it? Are there any sports, hobbies, or other activities in your culture that might be misunderstood and negatively valued by other cultures?

But, realistically, we can't probe every single activity in every culture to try to understand them. Can we perhaps find a limited number of features that will help us to understand our own culture and other tribes' cultures?

To do this, we will use the results of a major research study which used 116,000 questionnaires collected from employees of the same multinational company in 39 countries. The conclusion of the study was that there are 'four main dimensions on which… cultures differ':[35]

- Power Distance
- Uncertainty Avoidance
- Individualism
- Masculinity.

Let's look at what was found under each of these dimensions. Your country may be one of the 39 that were examined, and you may be surprised by the findings (or perhaps you will have your analysis confirmed!).

POWER DISTANCE
We have already looked briefly at the issue of social stratification and might agree that 'some societies have elaborate formal systems of dominance; others go to great lengths to de-emphasise dominance (including, for example, dominance in relationships between parent and child, teacher and student, boss and subordinate)'.[36]

The research project looked specifically at the latter kind of relationship and measured the difference between the extent to which the boss can determine the behaviour of the subordinate and the extent to which the subordinate can determine the behaviour of the boss. The conclusion is that this distance is 'to a considerable extent determined by... national culture'.[37]

The results, ranked from the highest to the lowest power distance, are given below. First, however, a word of caution about this, and all, quantitative descriptions of culture. No culture should be reduced to a 'score' and no number can capture the diversity of the human spirit. Nevertheless, it can be of practical use to measure cultural difference if we use this awareness to enhance our sensitivity to one another. With due caution, therefore, here are the results.[38] Remember: the higher the score, the greater the power distance.

Philippines	94	Japan	54
Mexico	81	Italy	54
Venezuela	81	South Africa	49
India	77	Argentina	49
Singapore	74	U.S.A.	40
Brazil	69	Canada	39
Hong Kong	68	Netherlands	38
France	68	Australia	36
Colombia	67	Germany (F.R.)	35
Turkey	66	Great Britain	35
Belgium	65	Switzerland	34
Peru	64	Finland	33
Thailand	64	Norway	31
Chile	63	Sweden	31
Portugal	63	Ireland	28
Greece	60	New Zealand	22
Iran	58	Denmark	18
Taiwan	58	Israel	13
Spain	57	Austria	11
Pakistan	55		

The maximum theoretically possible result (in which every person surveyed gives answers which indicate the most extreme power distance) would be 210. Conversely, the lowest possible score (with every person surveyed selecting answers which exhibited the least power distance) would be –90.

If your country was not included in the research, where would you place it in this ranking?

As with any bottom-line total, these scores do in some cases disguise considerable *internal* diversity. When the research study looked at the perceptions of different categories of subordinates (for example, skilled vs. unskilled) within each national group, it found quite a range in some countries (for example in Great Britain), but very little internal variation in others (for example, in India). Here are a few examples of this internal diversity:[39]

	A	a	b	c	d
Great Britain	35	15	50	42	102
Canada	39	24	42	55	80
India	77	80	81	87	88

A = the power distance perceived across all occupations within the national group

a = the power distance perceived by branch office technical experts, average educational level 15.8 years

b = the power distance perceived by head office clerks, average educational level 12.9 years

c = the power distance perceived by branch office service technicians, average educational level 12.2 years

d = the power distance perceived by unskilled plant workers, average educational level 10.5 years

What are the implications of greater or lesser power distance? A wide range of social phenomena associated with power distance were surveyed and some of these are listed below (#1–11).[40] As you read them, you might ask yourself whether they correlate with *high* or *low* power distance.

1. The government tends to be more autocratic.
2. There are large wage differentials.
3. There is a relatively small proportion of supervisory personnel.
4. The tax system aims to redistribute wealth.
5. There tends to be greater domestic political violence.
6. Students tend to have positive associations with 'power' and 'wealth'.
7. Higher-educated employees hold much less authoritarian values than lower-educated ones.
8. Employees feel it is possible to disagree with their boss.
9. People feel that powerholders are entitled to privileges.

10. If political parties exist, there is a polarisation between left and right, with a weak centre.

11. People feel that the way to change a social system is by overthrowing those in power.

(Answer: The research indicates that characteristics # 1, 2, 5, 6, 9, 10 and 11 correlate with greater power distance.)

Clearly, different perceptions of power distance will have considerable impact in intercultural communication. Consider the implications of different power-distance values in a multicultural office or in an intercultural business meeting:

- How will bosses get workers to do something in a low-power-distance culture?
- How might a high-power-distance boss be regarded if she managed people from low-power-distance cultures?
- Would you expect workers to use familiar or formal terms of address when talking to their boss in a high-power-distance culture?
- If a high-power-distance worker is listening to his boss give instructions, what kind of body language might he use?
- Other cultures may have a different perspective on power distance (between bosses and workers, for example).

OBSERVATION CHECKLIST

The following list is only a small sample of the kind of things you might observe about power distance — in your own culture and in other cultures:

- Is industrial action, such as going on strike, common?
- Do people openly acknowledge different social classes in the tribe?
- Do workers contribute to decision-making in the workplace?

UNCERTAINTY AVOIDANCE

People in all societies face uncertainty. They try to cope with the inevitable uncertainty of existence through the imposition of law or social convention, through religion, and through a set of attitudes.

However, the *degree* to which they will seek certainty will differ from tribe to tribe. If you (and your tribe) prefer things to be fixed and clear-cut, to see things in black and white, if you like stability and are disinclined to change, then your uncertainty avoidance is high.

In the workplace, the research project looked at three aspects of uncertainty avoidance: compliance with rules, stability in employment, and levels of stress, noting: 'When the mean anxiety level of a country is higher, people feel more stressed; but at the same time they try to cope with the anxiety by a greater need for security, which is visible in both rule orientation and employment stability.'[41]

Where do you think your culture will rank? If your culture is not in the survey, you might like to choose a few countries from the list and predict their rankings. Here are the results:[42]

Greece	112	Thailand	64
Portugal	104	Iran	59
Belgium	94	Finland	59
Japan	92	Switzerland	58
Peru	87	Netherlands	53
France	86	Australia	51
Chile	86	Norway	50
Spain	86	South Africa	49
Argentina	86	New Zealand	49
Turkey	85	Canada	48
Mexico	82	U.S.A.	46
Israel	81	Philippines	43
Colombia	80	India	40
Venezuela	76	Great Britain	35
Brazil	76	Ireland	35
Italy	75	Hong Kong	29
Pakistan	70	Sweden	29
Austria	70	Denmark	23
Taiwan	69	Singapore	8
Germany (F.R.)	65		

This time the highest theoretical possible score was +230, with the lowest –150.

Within these results for each country there may be significant differences for age, with different levels of uncertainty avoidance in different age groups. When the results are statistically controlled for age, there are in some cases significant increases in the score (for example, Japan, Hong Kong and Singapore rise to 112, 61, and 31, respectively); in other cases, there are drops (for example, Norway falls to 38), but the majority of the scores differ only very slightly.

Again, the research study looked at the expression of high or low uncertainty avoidance in a range of social phenomena.[43] What predictions would you make in the following? Do they correlate with *high* or *low* uncertainty avoidance?

1. Nationalism is relatively strong.
2. There are lower speed limits and fewer fatal road accidents.

3. There is more structuring of activities.
4. There are fewer nurses per doctor.
5. There is more tolerance for citizen protest.
6. Competition between employees is emotionally disapproved of.
7. Loyalty to the employer is seen as a virtue.
8. There is a preference for broad guidelines, rather than clear requirements and instructions.
9. There is more emotional resistance to change.
10. The average age in senior-level jobs is quite high.
11. Conflict in organisations is considered desirable.

(Answer: The research indicates that characteristics #1, 2, 3, 6, 7, 9 and 10 correlate with higher uncertainty avoidance.)

Given differences in uncertainty avoidance, again, what are the implications for bilateral business meetings or multicultural workplaces?

✍ Other cultures may have a different predisposition to uncertainty avoidance.

OBSERVATION CHECKLIST

The following list is only a small sample of the kind of things you might observe about uncertainty avoidance — in your own culture and in other cultures:

- Do people tend to move jobs and move house (assuming there is a reasonable level of opportunity available)?
- In general, is risk-taking regarded positively or negatively?
- Is there some degree of admiration for people who break the rules?

INDIVIDUALISM

Here, societies are measured for the relative emphasis on individualism or on collectivism, that is, the 'emotional dependence on (or independence from) groups, organisations, or other collectivities'.[44]

The general statement is that 'in some societies, individualism is seen as a blessing and a source of well-being; in others, it is seen as alienating'.[45]

The tendency is that a high degree of individualism correlates with low power distance (see above), but this is not always the case: for example, the Latin European countries score high on individualism but they also score high on power distance.

In examining individualism/collectivism, the research study found that the central element in determining relative individualism versus collectivism is our *self-concept*. How did you answer the self-identification question on page 39? Do you think your answer might be common in your tribe (and will correlate with the research findings on individualism versus collectivism for your culture)?

Concepts of personality are relevant here. There are a range of such concepts, including the view from a Chinese scholar that the Western concept of 'personality', seen as a separate entity distinct from society and culture, does not exist in the Chinese tradition.[46]

Individualism/collectivism is worthy of comment, as it appears in my personal experience to be a particularly powerful source of cross-cultural criticism:

- Individualistic cultures who regard collectivist cultures negatively, seeing those cultures as mindlessly suppressing the individual would do well to consider the following assessment: 'maintaining the group's well-being is the best guarantee for the individual'.[47]

- Conversely, collectivist cultures who see individualistic cultures as selfish, inconsiderate and dispassionate, would do well to understand that these societies have similar concerns as their own, but use a reverse strategy, that is: a focus on 'healthy' individuals will ensure the collective well-being.

The results of the study are given below:[48]

U.S.A.	91	India	48
Australia	90	Japan	46
Great Britain	89	Argentina	46
Canada	80	Iran	41
Netherlands	80	Brazil	38
New Zealand	79	Turkey	37
Italy	76	Greece	35
Belgium	75	Philippines	32
Denmark	74	Mexico	30
Sweden	71	Portugal	27
France	71	Hong Kong	25
Ireland	70	Chile	23
Norway	69	Singapore	20
Switzerland	68	Thailand	20
Germany (F.R.)	67	Taiwan	17
South Africa	65	Peru	16
Finland	63	Pakistan	14
Austria	55	Colombia	13
Israel	54	Venezuela	12
Spain	51	● Theoretical range: 100–0.	

Once more, predict the associated characteristics. Do the following (#1–11)[49] equate with *high* or *low* individualism?

1. People seek a moral (rather than a calculative) involvement with their company.
2. Social relations tend to be predetermined in terms of in-groups.
3. More importance is attached to training and use of skills in jobs.
4. More importance is attached to freedom and challenge in jobs.
5. Managers rate having security more important.
6. Managers rate having autonomy more important.
7. There tends to be more press freedom.
8. Promotion from inside is common.
9. Employees expect the organisation to defend their interests.
10. Policies and practices should allow for individual initiative.
11. Policies and practices should be based on loyalty and sense of duty.

(Answer: The research indicates that characteristics #4, 6, 7, and 10 correlate with more individualistic societies.)

- What might happen if an open-plan office design is forced on workers from an individualistic culture?
- Given what you read about Australian Aboriginals on page 37, would you describe their culture as relatively individualistic or collectivist?

OBSERVATION CHECKLIST
The following list is only a small sample of things you might observe about individualism and collectivism — in your own culture and in other cultures.

- Do people live alone (by choice)?
- Do people go places alone or do they ask someone to accompany them?
- Are people concerned about disturbing others when they are sleeping?
- Would most people prefer to travel independently or in an organised tour-group?
- Other cultures may see the relationship between the individual and the collective differently from you.

MASCULINITY
In order to determine whether a particular culture is more masculine or more feminine, there are two assumptions[50] in the research project:

(i) The statistically predominant socialisation pattern world-wide is for men to be more assertive and for women to be more nurturing and socially interdependent.

(ii) In the workplace women place emphasis on a friendly atmosphere, position security, their relationship with the manager, cooperation, and physical conditions. Men stress advancement, earnings, and training.

If a significant number of men in a society display preferences which are more conventionally associated with women (using the two assumptions given above), then that society will score low on the masculinity index.

Try to predict your tribe's ranking (or the ranking of other tribes). Here are the results:[51]

Japan	95		Canada	52
Austria	79		Pakistan	50
Venezuela	73		Brazil	49
Italy	70		Singapore	48
Switzerland	70		Israel	47
Mexico	69		Turkey	45
Ireland	68		Taiwan	45
Great Britain	66		Iran	43
Germany (F.R.)	66		France	43
Philippines	64		Spain	42
Colombia	64		Peru	42
South Africa	63		Thailand	34
U.S.A.	62		Portugal	31
Australia	61		Chile	28
New Zealand	58		Finland	26
Greece	57		Denmark	16
Hong Kong	57		Netherlands	14
Argentina	56		Norway	8
India	56		Sweden	5
Belgium	54			

Theoretical range: 100–0.

When the results are statistically controlled for the percentage of women in the survey, some results go up (for example, Finland increases to 51 and Greece to 73), some decrease (Japan moves to 87, although this is still the highest), but most exhibit little change.

Consider the following characteristics[52] and decide how they correlate with the masculinity score (high or low):

1. There is a strong belief in group decisions.
2. Work is less central in people's lives.
3. People prefer more salary to shorter working hours.
4. There is higher job stress.

5. There tends to be greater sex role equality in children's books.
6. Students are more benevolent (showing sympathy for the weak and disadvantaged).
7. There is less occupational segregation: e.g. there are more male nurses.
8. Organisational interests are a legitimate reason for interfering with people's private lives.
9. Slower car driving and fewer accidents.
10. Women occupy fewer more qualified and better-paid jobs.
11. The country (if wealthy) gives more aid.

(Answer: The research indicates that characteristics #3, 8 and 10 correlate with more masculine societies.)

What are the implications for the workplace?

- If you were opening a branch of your company in a very 'feminine' society, what steps might you take to increase worker satisfaction?
- If you were opening a branch of your company in a very 'masculine' society, what steps might you take to increase worker satisfaction?

OBSERVATION CHECKLIST

The following list is only a small sample of the kind of things you might observe in your own culture and in other cultures:

- Does the society have a strong welfare system (economy permitting)?
- Is there an attempt at distribution of wealth through different income-tax rates?
- Are minority groups within the tribe protected and supported?
- Is 'job satisfaction' important (regardless of rank or salary)?
- Cultures may have more 'masculine' or feminine' characteristics than your own.

This concludes a brief overview of the research study. According to this study, how would you describe *your* culture?

Values are not universal. If, however, you believe that your (culture's) preference, your way of deciding what is good, what is right, what is appropriate, what is polite, is the *only* way or the *correct* way — failing to acknowledge that there are other ways, which are valid for other people — then your attitude is 'ethnocentric'. Similarly, if you understand and evaluate other cultures *in terms of your own*, this is equally ethnocentric.

- Once upon a time a marmoset decided to leave the forest and explore the great, wide world. He travelled to the city and saw many strange and wonderful things but finally he decided to return home. Back in the forest, his friends and relatives crowded round. 'Well,' they cried, 'what did you see?' 'I saw buildings made of concrete and glass. Buildings so high that they touched the sky,' said the marmoset. And all of his friends and relatives imagined glass branches scratching the sky. 'The buildings were full of people walking on two legs and carrying briefcases,' said the marmoset. And his friends and relatives could almost see the people running along the branches with their tails wrapped firmly around their briefcases.[53]

Have a look at the following statements/beliefs. Which ones do you think are likely to be ethnocentric?

1. You should look people in the eye when you're talking.
2. Mothers should do everything possible to take care of their children.
3. Bowing to someone shows politeness and respect.
4. When you attend a social function, you should introduce yourself to the other guests.
5. 'What's your Christian name?'
6. 'What's your first name?'
7. Wives should obey their husbands.
8. When a group of friends eat out together, one person should pay for everybody.
9. Teachers should dress politely.
10. Bosses shouldn't reprimand their staff.
11. People become adults when they are eighteen years old.
12. Conflicts between children and parents are natural.
13. You shouldn't take cold drinks if you have a cold.
14. People feel envious when they see someone drive past in a luxury car.
15. You don't need to contact friends before visiting them.

All of the statements (with the probable exception of #2) are ethnocentric — that is, they contain a culture-specific assumption. Of the fifteen statements, perhaps only #6 needs a comment, as you may have assumed that having a first name is universal. In fact, it is not — quite a number of Indonesians, for example, use only one name, and therefore do not have a 'first name' and 'family name'.

- ✖ This is normal.
- ⊘ This is what I/we believe is normal. It may not be true in all cultures.
- ✖ That's impolite.
- ⊘ That is what I/we regard as impolite. It may not be so in all cultures.
- ✖ You should always look people in the eye when you're talking.
- ⊘ I/we believe that you should always look people in the eye when you are talking. It may not be the case in all cultures.

Again and again, when we look across cultures, we see people either (i) trying to achieve different goals, or (ii) trying to achieve the same goals, but using different means. To be aware of this is one of the major steps towards intercultural awareness.

We've seen examples of different goals (playing a good badminton game versus playing a good tennis game, so to speak). What about same goals, different means? If you have access to people from, say, three different cultures, ask them to describe their people. Do similar descriptions emerge, such as 'friendly' and 'kind'? If so, can we assume that they achieve these things in the same way?

Try this as a straightforward example. Would you agree that in most cultures people would try to help a friend who is unhappy — that is, they share the same goal? OK? Here are at least three different ways of achieving that goal. Which is closest to your tribe's way?

- Show them you are concerned and want to help. Ask them detailed questions about the problem so you can understand it as fully as possible. Then give the person the best possible advice you can. Try to be specific. Explain your advice, showing how it is based on your own experience and knowledge. Urge the person as best you can to take action so that the problem will be solved. Be as constructive and positive as possible.

- Show them as much sympathy as possible, making it clear to them that you really feel sorry for them. Gradually, try to cheer the person up, getting them to look on the bright side and assuring them that the problem will be solved. If possible, try to distract the person by gradually changing the topic and getting them involved in some enjoyable activity. Be as friendly and cheerful as possible.

- Encourage them to speak about their problem and listen very carefully. Try to get them to talk as much as possible, echoing what they say so they have a chance to decide for themselves what the best solution would be. Don't judge them and don't try to advise them how to solve the problem. Also, make them understand that you really can understand how they feel because you have had similar experiences. Be as supportive as possible.

Now, go beyond 'being helpful' and apply this same principle to 'being good', 'being successful', 'being polite', and so on — and we're on our way.

We have looked briefly at the kinds of value systems, perceptions, and social systems that underlie cultures. These are the underpinnings of societies and of the individual. We have seen individuals coming to different (usually unconscious) agreements with the other members of their tribe about virtually every aspect of existence: how to manage their bodies; how to think logically; how to express emotion; how to give important information about the world when they speak; how to decide what is appropriate behaviour; how to ascribe value to people and things — in short, how to be.

Emerging as critical intercultural skills are the abilities to distance ourselves from our own assumptions and to acknowledge that, in the world's cultures, both the ends and the means towards those ends can vary enormously.

'It is somewhat difficult for us to recognise that the value which we attribute to our own civilisation is due to the fact that we participate in this civilisation, and that it has been controlling our actions since the time of our birth; but it is certainly conceivable that there may be other civilisations, based perhaps on different traditions and on a different equilibrium of emotion and reason, which are of no less value than ours, although it may be impossible for us to appreciate their values without having grown up under their influence.'[54]

Before we turn to our second central issue, how people communicate, let's review where we have reached in our action list.

ACTION LIST

✍ Remember, cultures manage their bodies differently, requiring different behaviours and imposing different constraints on physical actions.

✍ Acknowledge that your language is not 'better' (more precise, more complex, more beautiful) than other languages.

✍ Understand that other cultures are not necessarily trying to achieve the same things as you. They may have different values.

✍ Understand that other cultures may be trying to achieve the same things as you, but may do so in very different ways.

✍ Accept that your own behaviour stems from a set of cultural values.

✍ Accept that your perceptions stem from a set of concepts and attitudes developed by your tribe. Your perceptions are biased and subjective.

✍ Remember that other cultures may have a different perspective on power distance (between bosses and workers, for example).

✍ Remember that other cultures may have a different predisposition to uncertainty avoidance.

✍ Other cultures may see the relationship between the individual and the collective differently from you.

✍ Above all, don't assume your way is *the* way. Be ready for different approaches.

'Excuse me, how best should I interrupt you?'

What are you trying to say?
Looking at communication

3

P ROBABLY the most important thing to understand about communication is this:

> When we communicate we always have a purpose. We don't just communicate for its own sake. We use language to *do things*. We use it to express our emotions and attitudes, to give our ideas and opinions, to complain, to gain acceptance or approval, to get information, to entertain, to build a relationship, to give advice, to fill in time, to instruct people, to ask for help, and so on.

This is universal: all tribes have pretty much these same fundamental communication needs. And, what's more, they have the same basic tools for communication: vocal organs, hands, faces, and bodies, and most tribes nowadays also have at least some of the tools available to extend communication: writing implements, microphones, computers, radios, t.v.s, cassettes, and so on.

So — the same fundamental needs, the same inclination to do things with language, and (more or less) the same communication tools. Where's the problem, then?

Well, if we are to succeed, we must do these things in *appropriate* ways, which of course is where culture — the arbiter of appropriacy — comes in. Over the generations, we have established 'rules' about how to communicate, and these rules will differ from tribe to tribe. To get you started, here are just a few communication matters to consider.

- When we talk, should we touch (stroke, kiss, fondle, shake hands with) each other?
- What should we call each other?
- Should we acknowledge or ignore difference and similarity amongst ourselves ('yes, sir', for example, versus 'sure, mate')?
- How do we get other people to do what we want?
- What 'space' (both in a concrete sense and an abstract sense) do we need to give each other when we talk?
- How much should we talk?
- Which emotions should we express (to whom, when, and how)?
- How can we get other people to accept and like us?
- Do we notice when someone is breaking the rules, either inadvertently or intentionally?
- Are there some things we can't talk about?

It sounds complicated — and it is — but we do most of it automatically. The linguistic system we are each brought up in is also complex, but most of us manage to master it and it becomes 'second nature'.

In this chapter, we'll look at some of the mechanics of communication, trying to see what we take for granted and do automatically. As you read, the first step is always to keep asking yourself what your own tribe's rules are. The second step is then to remind yourself that your way is no more and no less than that — *your* way.

And remember: the consequences of poor intercultural communication can range from the minor (and sometimes quite amusing) to the very serious, even tragic.

In turn, we'll look at:

- *body language* (how we use our faces and bodies to communicate)
- *address systems* (what we call one another)
- *openings and closings* (how we start and finish our conversations)
- *topic choice* (what we talk about)
- *helping and advising* (how we interact with people who need assistance)
- *turn control* (how we manage to take turns when we speak)
- *quantity and style of talk* (how much we should talk and how we should do it)
- *paying attention* (how we show that we're listening)
- *apologising* (when do we say we're sorry and how do we do it)
- *complimenting* (how we compliment each other and how we should react)
- *self-presentation* (what we do when we are trying to put our best foot forward)
- *politeness and 'face'* (what do we have to do to be considered polite)
- *negotiating* (how do we get what we want)
- *presenting information* (what's the best way of getting facts and viewpoints across)

One general point before we begin. Whenever we try to generalise about an aspect of communication, we'll often find ourselves saying 'well, it depends'. And that's exactly right. Communication *always* depends. Usually it depends on three factors:

- the relationship between the people involved;
- the purpose of the communication; and
- the context (the location and the circumstances of the situation).

That said, let's have a look at communication, moving from the concrete and visible through to the highly abstract and invisible.

WHAT ARE YOU TRYING TO SAY?

BODY LANGUAGE

Firstly, we often use our bodies (through gesture) to directly communicate our meaning. This can vary enormously from culture to culture. For example, what gestures (augmented perhaps by sounds) does your tribe use to convey the following ideas?

- yes
- come here
- delicious
- good luck
- expensive
- look at that

- no
- so-so: not good, not bad
- crazy
- be quiet
- intelligent
- I don't know

Are there things on this list that you don't have commonly recognised gestures for in your culture? If you have access to people from other cultures, ask them to perform these communications for you. You may be astonished! If you have no opportunity to get information from other tribes, here are a couple of examples, to give you a feel for the diversity of body language:

- The Iranians, among others, commonly jerk their heads upwards and click their tongues when they are talking. In my tribe, this would be an expression of disgust. For Iranians, it is a perfectly polite way of indicating 'no' (which my tribe indicates by a sideward shake of the head, a gesture which Iranians, in turn, would understand to mean 'I don't know'!).

- I had been living in Hong Kong for quite a few months and had eaten quite a few meals with Chinese people before I realised that they were thanking restaurant waiters by unobtrusively tapping the table with their fingers. How easy it would have been to jump to the inaccurate conclusion that Chinese restaurant guests never acknowledge service! ('What rude people!')

Body language is endlessly fascinating. How, for example, can you point at something without using your arms or hands? No problem. Quite a lot of tribes do it by raising the head and looking in the direction of the thing and, for extra emphasis, pursing the lips. (By the way, do be careful about pointing at *people* cross-culturally. It can be a very sensitive issue: there are often restrictions on whether you should point at all, and if so, how you should do it.)

Of course, body language does more than just convey particular meanings. We may use our bodies to make contact with the other person when we speak —

perhaps for emphasis, or to maintain their attention, or express our relationship. On the other hand, some tribes may touch only rarely when they speak!

- One research study[1] looked at the number of times couples touched each other in cafes in different cities. This is what they found:

(a) San Juan, Puerto Rico: 180   times per hour
(b) Paris, France: 110   times per hour
(c) London, England: 0   times per hour

What might happen when (a) and (c) communicate? Certainly, if they assume their way is *the* way, there could be some difficulties.

It seems reasonable to say that there are *high-contact* and *low-contact* cultures (and of course those in between). How would you rate your tribe on this dimension?

Thirdly, and most importantly, we use our bodies to signal our feelings, attitudes and reactions to other people when we communicate. In fact, one researcher found that more than sixty-five per cent of the social meaning of a typical two-person exchange is conveyed by non-verbal cues (that is, body language).[2]

Do people read this communication accurately across cultures? The results of research are not encouraging.

- One researcher filmed a group of American men and women who were asked to indicate agreement and courtesy during their communication.[3] The film was then shown to groups of people in Beirut, Tokyo, and Bogota. These groups were quite unable to 'read' the American attempts to convey these basic aspects of communication.

- Another study asked groups of Italians, Japanese and English people to read one another's (and their compatriots') emotions and interpersonal attitudes, judging from face and voice.[4] The results are given below, the scores indicating the percentage of accurate 'readings'. So, looking at the first line of results, for example, the English were right 61% of the time when they were looking at the body language of fellow English people, but only 55% correct and 36% correct when looking at Italians and Japanese, respectively.

| | Performers | | |
	English	Italian	Japanese
English	61	55	36
Italian	52	62	29
Japanese	54	56	43*

Judges (left label)

*One explanation for the surprising result from the Japanese is that the subtlety of facial expression causes difficulty even within their own tribe.

Eye-contact while speaking can vary enormously from culture to culture, with some tribes requiring it and others avoiding it. Or they may use eye contact for different *purposes*.

- One study which compared the use of eye contact between English people and South Asians concluded that the South Asians use gaze to monitor reactions, determine whose turn it is to speak, and to call attention to new information. English people, on the other hand, seek the other person's gaze when they are addressing them or listening to what they are saying.[5]

Body language in greetings is also a complex area.

- In the early months of living in Iran I observed how men greeted each other. Regardless of the frequency of contact, it seemed that men needed to perform a greeting ritual which seemed more complex than that in my own culture. This ritual involved quite a lot of body language, including shaking hands (sometimes embracing and kissing — I didn't have the rules for this yet), putting the right hand to the heart (to indicate sincerity?), smiling, and a sideways inclination of the head. As for what was spoken during this greeting, there seemed to be questions about health and family. I started to participate in the ritual, with non-Western-influenced Iranians (Western-experienced Iranian men would greet me in English and shake hands). In performing my greetings, I noticed that I could mumble just about anything I liked (which was just as well, because I wasn't yet confident with the language) but, as long as I participated in the body language, things seemed to go off very well. I wonder if the reverse — accurate language but inappropriate body language — would have been as successful? Years later, this early experience would be useful in Indonesia, in greeting (especially Muslim) men. Many elements were similar — the handshake, the smile, the touching of the heart — and again, what you actually said seemed relatively less important.

Finally, some cultures have a number of constraints with regard to the body that you should be aware of. Particularly common taboos are (i) to avoid using the left hand for passing things, handing things out, or even eating and drinking; (ii) to avoid touching someone's head; and (iii) to avoid pointing your foot at someone.

- All cultures impose some constraints on the body.
- Different rules about appropriate use of the body can lead to intercultural misunderstandings.

ADDRESS SYSTEMS

Suppose a man's name is Karim (first name) Metwali (family name). How would you address him? Would you call him:

1. 'Karim'
2. 'Mr Karim'
3. 'Mr Metwali'
4. 'Mr Karim Metwali' or
5. 'Metwali'?

Are there any other possibilities instead of 'Mr'? Do you need to know anything about him (for example, his age or his profession) before you know how to address him? How many ways are possible? Which ways would be accepted by your tribe, and which, if any, rejected? In my tribe, only alternatives 1 and 3, and possibly 4, are permitted when addressing a person.

Cultures often use titles in referring to particular professions, holders of certain educational (or other) achievements, or holders of certain social status:

- In my tribe, for example, we use professional titles in talking to and referring to certain members of the medical profession and for holders of PhD degrees (actually, the titles are the same for the two groups, causing quite a lot of confusion in our tribe!). We also use titles for certain holders of religious office, and for certain members of the nursing profession, and we use status titles for certain women and men who have inherited or been awarded a particular status by the country's monarch. In Indonesia, I will use titles in referring to certain members of the medical profession and for PhD holders (fortunately, the two are distinct, so there is no confusion, but I do have to remember which is which!), for holders of Master's degrees (and here I have to make a gender distinction), holders of higher degrees in engineering, for certain holders of religious office, and for people who have completed the pilgrimage to Mecca (with, again, a gender difference).

What do you do in your culture?

Also, naming systems can vary enormously from culture to culture.

- When, many years ago I was working as an interpreter on a Russian ship, my Russian colleagues did not feel comfortable calling me 'Kerry'. They asked my father's name (Patrick) and from that point on I was invariably called Kerry Patrickovich, conforming to their standard system of using first name and 'patronymic'. What would you be called by a Russian? Be careful: if you're a woman, you add '-ovna' to your father's name. So, my sister would be Helen Patrickovna. (Actually, she'd have to be Helen*a* Patrickovna, as all female names, both first names and family names, must end in '-a', as in Rais_a_ Gorbachev_a_.) Language and culture are fascinating, aren't they? But back to the business of how to address people.

If, in your tribe, you want to call the attention of a stranger — let's say they are walking in front of you and they have dropped something — how would you do it? Will you make distinctions according to gender, age, or status? Or perhaps some other variable? Will you avoid using a title and instead use some other way of calling the person's attention — simply say 'Excuse me', for example? How would you call the attention of a waiter/waitress in a restaurant? Are the rules the same as with the 'stranger on the street' example? (Do be careful: some terms of address for waiters do not transfer well into other languages and cultures. Terms such as 'Boy' or 'You', for example, may not be well received.)

How do subordinates and bosses, teachers and students (at various levels of education), parents and children, siblings, neighbours, colleagues tend to address each other? Is it possible to shift the address system after a period of time? (For example, 'Oh, please call me Jan'). If so, who initiates this and how do they do it?

If you are an English speaker who uses the title 'Ms', how would you explain it to someone outside your culture, who has learnt that the system in English only allows for a choice between 'Mrs' and 'Miss'? (Being a teacher of culture can be quite tricky, can't it?)

In general, address systems can be a maze. There is no easy way to learn their complexities. Frankly, the best advice I can give is:

- Keep asking for advice about what to call people. There will generally be somebody who can get you started in the right direction.

Also, there are two other general guidelines to consider:

- Don't automatically follow the address systems you hear. The people of the tribe might not find it appropriate to integrate you into their systems.

For example: Thais will, depending on the relative status and the context, often call a younger person '*Nong*' (younger sibling). Yet in all the years I have been speaking Thai, only one older person has consistently called me this — and he lives in America! Perhaps my status as a lecturer overrides the possibility of being called younger brother (once people know that I am a teacher, I am invariably called 'Teacher' or 'Teacher Kerry') — or perhaps it is simply that I am an outsider and it just doesn't make sense to incorporate me into the system. If people are not aware of my profession, they use the polite neutral '*Khun* Kerry'.

- Don't take offence — getting the form of address 'wrong' is rarely intended to be offensive.

In Thailand and Indonesia, you may often hear people trying to get a

Westerner's attention by calling 'Hey, you' and 'Hey, Mister', respectively. Focus on what they're trying to *do* (i.e. to call your attention) not on how they're doing it. (Incidentally, if you are a native speaker of English, how would you go about explaining to an Indonesian that 'Hey, Mister' can be offensive, but 'Hey, Mister Johnson' is fine! Or that 'Excuse me, Missus' breaks a rule, whereas 'Excuse me, Miss' is acceptable. Good luck.)

OPENING AND CLOSING

All communication encounters — whether formal or informal, face-to-face or distant — have some kind of opening and some kind of closing.

For example, telephone conversations require some kind of opening and closing, and this can be quite difficult when operating in other languages and cultures. Don't just transfer from your own 'script': for example, just because you know how to say 'hello' in Thai doesn't necessarily mean you should use it on the phone. That may not be their conventional routine. Indeed, different cultures use a wide range of routines to answer a call (for example, Russians commonly say '(I'm) listening'). There will also be differences in the way they identify themselves (some cultures say 'With Kerry', equivalent to the English 'This is Kerry' or 'Kerry speaking').

Also critical is what we call the 'pre-closing move', the signal we give to indicate to the other person that we are ready to close the call: English speakers, for example, might say something like 'Well, I'd better let you go' or 'OK, so you'll send me that fax tomorrow, yeah?'. Needless to say, pre-closing moves can be quite tricky cross-culturally, and the exchange may feel quite awkward if an inappropriate signal is given or misinterpreted.

Of course, things can go wrong, as illustrated in this anecdote reported on 25 May 1993 in the *South China Morning Post*. (Intercultural mishaps don't always have to be serious. They can be quite amusing.)

> *Receptionist:* Good morning can I help you.
> *Caller:* Yes, please may I speak to Mr Bond?
> *R:* Yes, who's calling?
> *C:* Mr Gibbons.
> *R:* Could you spell that, please?
> *C:* Yes. G.I.B.B.O.N.S.
> *R:* Mr Giv —
> *C:* No, Mr GIBBONS, with two Bs, as in Bye Bye.
> *R:* Bye bye!
> (*Phone goes dead.*)

Intercultural telephone calls can range from the amusingly off-key, as in this example, to the disastrous — especially if the subject of the call is critical, such as responding to a job advertisement. Out of all of the above, what do you think you need to learn about the linguistic/cultural 'rules' of another culture's telephone calls. Where might the difficulties occur? If you are operating in another language, I would advise learning a number of standard routines used by native speakers of that language. This won't solve all the problems, but it will give you a reasonable framework.

How do face-to-face interactions compare with what we have seen for telephone calls? Do they have similar stages and similar routines? With regard to openings and closings in face-to-face interactions — which are, after all quite important — here are some of the things you might need to observe. Answer each one for your own tribe.

Firstly, how do you join a group of people who are already talking? What should you do and what should the members of the group do? What factors (such as age, status, setting, degree of familiarity) might influence the behaviour? Here are some conclusions from researchers about how people join in conversations in two different cultures:

- 'Young Germans rarely formally acknowledge the joining of a newly arrived person to their interaction.'[6]

- 'In Antigua no opening is necessarily made for a person joining a group in conversation; nor is there any pause or other formal signal that he is being included. No one appears to pay any attention. When he feels ready he will simply begin speaking. He may be heard, he may not.'[7]

Next, how are conversations opened? Does it matter who opens first? What routines are commonly used?

- One writer commented that the standard English comment about the weather to open the conversation is regarded as 'somewhat mentally retarded' by the Germans![8]

Are the responses expected to be formulaic, for example, do English speakers, when asked 'How are you?', respond with a medical update or merely say 'Fine'? Are the parties expected to reciprocate the routine?

- The same writer notes that English speakers usually reciprocate the 'How are you?' question with 'What about you?', whereas Germans don't — and that this lack of reciprocation would 'most likely appear inconsiderate and selfish' to the English speaker.[9]

In a first encounter with people what is the pattern of topic development? One example of topic development might be to move from the impersonal, to the mutual, to the personal — at a party, say, you might first talk about the food, then later about shared likes (you both like Thai food), and then, later still, ask each other's name and occupation. Of course, some tribes will have a totally different pattern of topic development than this.

What effect does setting have on how you open conversations? For example, would it matter if you met a compatriot at work, in an airport lounge, or in a foreign country?

Do business exchanges (popping into a colleague's office, say, or conducting a meeting) have a short lead-in or a long lead-in? Do you get straight to the point or do you 'warm up' first? Is there a lead-in when opening a service transaction (such as opening a new account at a bank)? Does the type of transaction affect the opening behaviour?

In conversations, do you identify yourself early in the exchange, delay this information, or wait for a third party to provide the introduction?

How do you present yourself? Do you, for example, include (unsolicited) information about your job or your employer?

- In Japan it is apparently common to give your work affiliation (your company or institution) as part of initial self-identity.

What information do you in turn solicit? Do you open more personal topics or delay? What does 'personal' mean, anyway? Does 'where you live' qualify as a 'personal' topic, for example?

How do you do a 'pre-closing move' (to signal that you are ready to finish the exchange)?

- In the Philippines it is apparently 'perfectly good manners to terminate a conversation on a public path by saying "You go now".'[10]

- One writer, speaking about the English culture, states that failure to perform or respond to a 'It's been nice talking to you' or 'Hope we meet again' routine could be interpreted as the complete rupture of the relationship.[11]

Finally, how do you close?

- English speakers have a 'See you (later, soon, around, etc)' routine. This is sometimes interpreted literally by people from other cultures, which can lead to misunderstandings. The meaning of 'Until we meet (again)', which is quite a common expression in a number of cultures is, on the other hand, relatively unambiguous.

For your own culture, you will be able to answer these questions, to some extent, merely by reflecting on past experience. In some cases, even this will probably not be enough to give you confident answers; observation will also be needed. In opening communication with people from *other* cultures, observation and analysis (looking for the right things and finding patterns) is even more critical.

Fortunately, many people in most cultures are flexible enough to cope with 'inappropriate' openings and closings.

🌿 How people open and close their conversations will differ culturally.

TOPIC CHOICE

Cultures vary according to the degree of acceptability/non-acceptability they assign to certain topics. In other words, there are some topics we would prefer to talk about and others we would prefer not to talk about, thank you very much. The following example may illustrate this for you.

Let's say a group of men and women, meeting for the first time at a professional conference, are chatting on the evening of the first day of the conference. After talking about the conference itself, their conversation starts to move towards other topics. The following is a list of potential topics. In your culture, what topics might they select? Rank them in order of acceptability and/or likelihood of selection. Are there any which they would probably avoid (because they are in some sense 'unacceptable') or simply fail to select (because there is little interest in that topic)?

1. One another's children
2. The weather
3. One another's religion
4. Some aspect of politics in the country
5. Their relative salaries
6. Problems in their professional field
7. The challenges in their profession
8. One another's marital status
9. Sexism in their professional field
10. Some recent gossip about the private life of the leader of the country

Naturally, even people within one culture will rank these topics differently, depending on personal experience and inclination, and on their interpretation of the context and its participants. If you are from my tribe, you may not agree with my overall ranking, but I feel confident that we will agree about the *least* likely topics. Here is my ranking (for my own culture): 7, 2, 4, 1, 6, 10, 9, 8, 5, 3. Does this differ very significantly from your own ranking?

● Recently I was conducting a language test interview. As part of this test, candidates are required to ask me about my accommodation and are given a set of prompt words to guide them in forming the questions ('location', 'outstanding features', 'facilities', and so on). One candidate, having worked her way partly through the list of prompt questions, began to quiz me about who lived in my house, what our relationship was, and how we arranged matters financially. Linguistically, no problem

— culturally, not so appropriate. (By the way, she was not penalised for cultural inappropriateness in her grade.)

In the following extract, the renowned Indonesian freedom fighter Trimurti is being interviewed. Notice how the interviewer, a Westerner speaking fluent Indonesian, pursues the topic of Trimurti's *feelings*. It appears that his expectation (his 'script', if you like) is for her to describe her feelings of despair and anger at her situation. She, however, avoids the topic almost entirely, perhaps because in her Javanese culture 'feelings' are not an acceptable topic for public disclosure.

I: Your child was in prison (with you) before he was one year old?

T: He was five-and-a-half months with me.

I: How did you feel about that?

T: How did I feel? I knew the risks of taking up the struggle.

I: Surely you felt something?

T: I took my baby there but he didn't stay. He was taken out by his father. But before I was released from prison his father was jailed. So the child was left with friends.

I: How did you feel when you heard that?

T: I wasn't worried because they were responsible people.

🕮 Cultures don't necessarily choose the same topics to talk about.

🕮 All cultures have some topics they would rather avoid.

TURN CONTROL

'Turn control' refers to the rules for taking turns in an exchange, for example in a conversation or a meeting.

Listed below are just some of the issues involved in taking turns. As you read them, it may help to imagine the same group of adult professionals chatting after the first day of a conference, which we considered above.

Is it normal and acceptable for people to 'jump in' while another is talking? How do they do it? Are there specific gestures, words or perhaps 'sounds' they use to try to take a turn or relinquish a turn? If there is a pause in the exchange, do people feel uncomfortable with this silence and try to fill it immediately?

● The rule in America appears to be this: 'At least one and not more than one party talks at a time.'[12] In other words, silence should be avoided. Too long a pause means that the other person is shy, or inattentive, or bored, or nervous. Someone has to speak to fill the gap. This is not necessarily true in other cultures, where people may feel perfectly comfortable with quite long silences. As for the second part of the rule, 'and not more than one', this means that there is little tolerance for too many people speaking at the same time. The 'layering' has to be resolved.

In your tribe, if one person's talk overlaps with another, do people feel uncomfortable and try to withdraw? Do they withdraw immediately or after quite a few seconds? Alternatively, do people feel quite comfortable with this layering of talk?

- 'In Antigua the start of a new voice is not in itself a signal for the voice speaking either to stop or to institute a process which will decide who is to have the floor.'[13]

- 'Turks are used to long monologues without interruption, together with more narrative than the Germans expect. Turks find it difficult to function effectively in a society with short exchanges. They are not accustomed to interjecting, nor do they take advantage of non-verbal cues for them to take their conversation turn.'[14]

Are there any unstated rules about who has precedence in turn-taking? Do factors such as relative age, gender, or relative status influence turn-taking, or do all the participants regard themselves as having equal rights as turn-takers?

- Among the Burundi people the order in which individuals speak in a public discussion is strictly determined by seniority of rank.[15]

The next time you have an opportunity, observe a group of adults from a culture other than your own (either in real life, or perhaps in a film or T.V. program). Don't worry about what they are saying: focus, instead, on their turn-taking behaviour. Try to answer some of the questions posed above. Do the rules appear very different from your own culture?

- Observe how other cultures join in and take turns in a conversation. The rules will probably be different from your own.

QUANTITY AND STYLE OF TALK

Although there appears to be little research supporting the claim, many people feel they are able to describe their tribe as being relatively talkative or reserved, compared with other tribes. For example, American people and English people tend, in my experience, to describe themselves as relatively talkative and reserved, respectively.

Certainly attitudes towards the *function* of 'talk' (and hence standards of quantity and style of talk) do appear to differ. Here, for example, is one comment by a Japanese scholar on his own culture's use of language:

- 'Language as an instrument of debate and argument is considered disagreeable and is accordingly avoided. It is only one possible means of communication, not *the* means of communication.'[16]

- Another author underscores this point by saying that 'the articulation of thoughts and feelings in oral language is often taken by the Japanese as an unmistakable sign that the speaker is neither profound nor sincere. For them, the world is not verbalizable nor is it aesthetically pleasing to try. Many native proverbs support this attitude: "mouths are to eat with, not to speak with", "A hundred listenings do not equal one seeing", "A man of many words has little refinement".'[17]

In your tribe, how much talk is expected during a meal, say? Is the pattern to eat and then talk, or to talk during the eating? Or some other pattern?

- I remember getting this wrong in one of the countries I lived in. I was having lunch with a group of new students and I was feeling that things were not going well. No matter how much I tried to initiate a chat, they seemed to avoid speaking to me. ('Going well' in my tribe would mean that we have a lively chat while we eat.) Fortunately, one of the students later explained that in their culture 'when you eat, you eat; when you speak, you speak'.

What about the quantity of talk in a job interview? Suppose this question were asked in an interview: 'Why have you applied for this job?'. For approximately how long would you expect the candidate to speak — less than a minute or more than a minute, say? (Incidentally, would this question be asked in a job interview in your culture?)

Suppose you were at a national conference. Several of your colleagues agree that one of the participants is a 'very good speaker'. What, more specifically, does that mean in your tribe? Does it, for example, mean that (a) she spoke for an appropriate amount of time, neither too little nor too much; (b) she presented her ideas in a very clear and organised manner; (c) she used the language very creatively, with word-plays, metaphors, etc; (d) she made some very clear conclusions; or (e) some other criteria? Are you a 'good speaker' by your tribe's standards?

- I remember when I went to America for postgraduate study. My first impression was that my American classmates spoke more in class than students in my tribe and were more articulate and self-confident. I felt very shy and didn't open my mouth. After some weeks I started to see through the quantity and style and was able to focus on the substance of their talk, which appeared to differ little from what I was used to. I started participating in the class exchanges.

Here are some insights into one culture's (again, the Japanese) value system with regard to 'talk':

'Precise and ordered talk may be considered odd and even "anti-social"; vagueness, indirectness and incompleteness are felt to be the necessary and appropriate method to structure verbal content.'[18]

An example of this style is given below:

'It isn't that we can't do it this way,' one Japanese will say. 'Of course,' replies his companion, 'we couldn't deny that it would be impossible to say that it couldn't be done.' 'But unless we can say that it can't be done', his friend adds, 'it would be impossible not to admit that we couldn't avoid doing it.'

Here is another style of talk, this time involving considerable redundancy, that is, repetition and rephrasing of information. The people in this culture appear to value a rhythmic two-or-three-repeat structure to their narratives. In this extract, the author of an autobiographical novel goes to a university in a region of the United States. She meets and is briefed by the senior woman in the girls' dormitory where she will live and work. This is how the woman begins to explain the job. (Of course this extract is written for literary effect, but I'm sure it does reflect one of the styles of talk found in this regional culture.)

'When a girl (in the dormitory) has a telephone call, you know what I mean, when the telephone rings, when somebody is calling her up. When a girl has a telephone call, you press her bell once. When she has a caller, when a boy comes in to get her, you know what I'm trying to say, when they've got a date that night and he picks her up, when he comes in and asks for her in person instead of calling on the phone, you understand what I mean. When she has a caller, then you press her bell twice. That way, she knows whether she's got a phone call or a caller. Because, see, if she has a caller and you press her bell once instead of twice, she'll think it's a call instead of a caller. She's come downstairs in her dressing gown with her hair up in curlers, and there stands her caller, just standing there right in front of her as big as life. She'd just die of embarrassment, you know what I mean, she'd just fall down dead is what I'm staying, she'd just perish!'[19]

When the author then meets a number of speakers who speak in a similar way, she realises that she is dealing with a culturally different communication style.

✍ Even allowing for individual differences, each culture probably has a distinctive 'communicative style'.

We'd better move on to the next topic, you know, the next thing on our list, otherwise we won't be getting ahead, we won't be moving forward, you know what I mean?

PAYING ATTENTION

It appears to be a universal of communication that listeners will signal to speakers that they are attending to what is being said. The strategies for paying attention, however, appear to vary considerably.

Here are just some of the ways of indicating that you are attending. Which (if any) of these does you tribe tend to favour:

- nodding the head
- looking directly into the speaker's eyes some, most, or all of the time he is speaking
- averting the eyes and placing the head in a way that the speaker will know that you are listening
- using appropriate sounds in the right places, such as 'uh-huh', 'oh?', tongue-clicking
- using words that show you are following the speaker's content, such as 'Really?', 'Did she?'
- completing, or echoing, the speaker's sentence
- remaining perfectly silent

What is one way of showing that you are paying attention in India and Sri Lanka? It is not on the list above. Answer: people rock their heads from side to side.

Interculturally, there can of course be misunderstandings when it comes to showing that you are attending. The speaker may feel that your attending strategies are excessive, inadequate, or simply inappropriate.

If you have the opportunity, observe a pair or group of speakers from another culture and see how they do it.

✍ Your way of showing that you are paying attention may be considered inappropriate by other cultures.

COMPLIMENTING

Although perhaps not a very frequent 'function' in communicating, it is useful to illustrate two points about communication.

Even though we may feel that we communicate in a very *individual* way, our way of doing things with language is actually rather uniform within each culture. For example:

- One research project analysed a total of 686 compliments gathered in a wide range of American English speech situations and found that only three patterns accounted for 85% of their data.[20] In other words, we perform the complimenting function in very standardised ways within our tribes.

There are, however, significant differences across cultures in how such functions as 'complimenting' are achieved. The differences are likely to involve: how explicit or indirect you should be; what constraints exist (how often, to whom, in what situations); and the content of the compliment itself.

- Here is an exchange between two Iranian friends, quoted by one researcher:[21]

  A: Your shoes are very nice.

  B: It is your eyes which can see them which are very nice.

In turn, responses to compliments may differ enormously. You may be required, alternatively, to thank, to deflect, to accept, or to vigorously deny the compliment. The example this time is taken from Indonesia:[22]

  A: You have a nice one-room apartment.

  B: Yes. The rent is expensive. It is a burden.

- An Indonesian I know was appalled, in his first months living in Australia, by the 'insincerity' of Australian complimenting behaviour. He noted that when going to somebody's house for the first time, people immediately complimented the owner on the house. Similarly, at meals, guests loaded their host(ess) with glowing praise for the quality of the food. He felt that none of this was sincere, and probably he was right, since much of this complimenting behaviour is a conventionalised routine in Australian culture.

Here is another common 'function' in communication in all cultures:

APOLOGISING

Again, cross-cultural differences will arise according to a number of variables:

- To whom should you apologise?
- In what situations is an apology required?
- How intense should the apology be?
- How should the apology be done?

Try this as an example. Which of the five alternatives listed below would you choose in the following situations?[23]

1 = no apology necessary
2 = weak apology necessary
3 = moderate apology necessary
4 = strong apology necessary
5 = very strong apology necessary

- You punish your young son for doing something wrong, but then you find out he didn't do it.

- You lose a friend's book.
- You break a friend's coffee cup.
- You spill your tea on the dining table during a meal at the boss's house.
- You arrive five minutes late for a business meeting.
- You bump into someone as you get off a bus.

Think of the variables which will influence your apologies in these examples. How do your answers reveal your tribe's values?

- When I gave this task to a group of postgraduate students from various cultures, the major divergence came with the example about apologising to your son. Some cultures scored this at 0–1, while others (such as my fellow Australians) felt that this would require an apology in the 3–5 range. (Mind you, my elderly mother gave it a 1–2, explaining that 'you wouldn't want your son to get the upper hand'!)

With the possible exception of my mother, Australians are, as one Chinese person commented, 'Always apologising, even to their family and close friends and for such small things! To me, it feels distant and unfriendly. I don't think you should have to be so polite to friends.'

REQUESTING, INVITING, OFFERING AND RESPONDING

If you look back to page 42, at the different values related to the parable of the two sons, you see two quite different views of what constitutes an appropriate response to a request. Which approach (value) did you choose?

Beyond this one small example is a wealth of difference in how cultures request, invite, and offer — and how they respond to all of these.

Generally speaking, how many times do you offer or invite, and how are you expected to respond?

- In my tribe, we appear to have a two-part structure. In each of the two phases, we have two alternative responses. For example:

  A: Would you like a drink?

  B: (1) *accept:* Thanks. That'd be great. *OR*

  (2) *decline:* No thanks. I just ...

  (If B has declined, we then check)

  A: Are you sure?

  B: (1) *confirm.* No thanks. Really, I ... *OR*

  (2) *reverse.* Well, OK. If .....

To go further than that might start to be regarded as pushy. How do other tribes manage this? Consider the following exchange:

  A: Would you like to come to a party at my place?

  B: Thank you.

What does the response mean? ('Thank you for the invitation' or 'Yes, I would like to come' or 'Thank you for the invitation but I'm unable to come'?). Do be careful: I have seen many intercultural misunderstandings because the speaker and the listener have assumed different interpretations. It is better to check.

I have found my own tribal behaviour for making and responding to offers, invitations, and requests not to be very useful when living in other cultures. In some cultures, these are the modifications I have made:

- In offering and inviting, I usually find I need to extend the number of times I make an offer or invitation.
- I tend to decline offers of goods and services until the person urges me to accept.
- For invitations, I put all my energy into thanking the person for the invitation, showing my appreciation. If the person seems to be looking for a clear response, I accept (and then some time later I may, if I prefer, withdraw). I have found a 'yes/but' approach is often more acceptable and successful than a 'no', especially when I have lived in non-Western cultures (if you will permit me such a gross generalisation).

All three of these behaviours differ from those in my tribe, which tends to value the respect of individual choice and 'directness' in responses. If you were interacting with my tribe, what modifications in your behaviour might you want to consider?

✍ All functions of communication, whether complimenting, apologising, requesting, inviting, or offering, proceed according to different cultural rules.

SELF-PRESENTATION

Self-presentation is, of course, not a separate 'function' in communication. Rather, it underlies *most* communication, influencing how we apologise, compliment, invite — indeed, how we perform many other, if not all, functions.

How do we present ourselves to, for example, a neighbour, a prospective mother-in-law, an interview panel, a colleague, or a stranger we meet at a party?

Self-presentation rests on two critical factors. Firstly, as we have already seen in Chapter 2, it is linked to our value system: what is appropriate; what is good; what is desirable in people's behaviour. Secondly, it is linked to our concept of politeness.

Often we tend to think politeness is restricted to certain more formal occasions. In fact, in the sense that I am using the word, 'politeness' is pervasive. It influences all our spoken and written communication, even in informal situations with people we know very well.

But let's start with a situation which more obviously calls for 'polite' communication — a job interview. Let's say you are in a job interview and the interviewer asks you: 'Do you think you can handle the management aspects of this position?' Here are two possibilities:

Culture (A)	Culture (B)
What do I have to do here?	*What do I have to do here?*
Show that I am a confident person!	*Show that I am a good and modest person!*
How will I achieve that?	*How will I achieve that?*
Choose the right words and gestures!	*Choose the right words and gestures!*
'Yes, I feel quite certain I can.'	'God willing, I will be able to do that.'
(Looks at the interviewer calmly and directly.)	*(Smiles self-deprecatingly and looks down.)*

The critical self-presentation decision here is determined by values: What is considered 'good' in this situation in this society — an expression of modesty or confidence, for example? What would be your goal in your culture and how might you go about achieving it? Would you be closer to A or to B, above?

What would you do in the following situations in your culture?

(a) The report which your assistant has submitted to you is one week late, incomplete, and of poor quality.

(b) You are chatting with an acquaintance. He is obviously enjoying the chat and wants to continue, but you're running late for your next appointment.

Which will prevail: your desire to be seen as a friendly polite person or your need to be seen as a reliably punctual (and therefore, polite) professional?

How would you present yourself in a situation where you are ten minutes late arriving at a formal meeting? Here are just two possibilities. Does either resemble your method of self-presentation (as a polite apologetic person)?

Culture (A)	Culture (B)
What do I have to do here?	*What do I have to do here?*
Show that I know I am late and am sorry.	*Show that I know I am late and am sorry.*
How will I achieve that? Choose the right words and gestures!	*How will I achieve that? Choose the right words and gestures!*
(Bows at the door and says) 'I'm sorry I'm late. I had to make a phone call' *(and goes to his seat).*	*(Goes directly to his seat and quietly says)* 'Excuse me.'

Notice that the two cultures here share the same value and are trying to achieve the same goal, but they do so in different ways.

Naturally, the introspective processes indicated above ('What do I have to do here?' and 'How can I achieve this'?) are in practice usually unconscious when operating within your own culture. The point is that, in successful intercultural communication, these analytical processes need to be made more conscious.

- Cultures have different goals in 'self-presentation' — that is, in the positive qualities about themselves they strive to present.
- Even if cultures have the same self-presentation goals, their ways of achieving these may differ.

HELPING AND ADVISING PEOPLE

To consider the issue of 'helping' in different cultures, we return to the example we first encountered on page 56. The three approaches to helping a friend with a problem are reproduced below. Which approach best describes what most people in your culture would tend to do in this situation? Probably all three cultures would have the same self-presentational goal: to be a good and useful friend. Beyond that, however, their goals may start to diverge, as would the means:

(a) Show them you are concerned and want to help. Ask them detailed questions about the problem so that you understand it as fully as possible. Then give the person the best possible advice you can. Try to be specific. Explain your advice, showing how it is based on your own experience and knowledge. Urge the person as well as you can to take action so that the problem will be solved. Be as constructive and positive as possible.

(b) Show them as much sympathy as possible, making it clear to them that you really feel sorry for them. Gradually, try to cheer the person up, getting them to look on the bright side and assuring them that the problem will be solved. If possible, try to distract the person by gradually changing the topic and getting them involved in some enjoyable activity. Be as friendly as possible.

(c) Encourage them to speak about their problem and listen very carefully. Try to get them to talk as much as possible, echoing and repeating what they say so that they have a chance to decide for themselves what the best solution would be. Don't judge them and don't try to advise them how to solve the problem. Also, make them understand that you really can understand how they feel because you have had similar experiences. Be as supportive as possible.

After you have chosen, consider this. While your choice may be influenced by such factors as your age, gender, and personality, there are, nevertheless, culture-specific patterns in the selection. Which selection do you think might be the most common in your culture? Do you accept that the two alternatives you *didn't* choose represent 'friendly' behaviour? Can you devise other approaches (to helping a friend with a problem)?

- Once when I was with a friend from a different culture I was feeling really down and he was putting enormous energy into changing the subject and cheering me up — in other words, he was using approach (b) above. It was having the opposite effect on me than the one intended. So I decided to be explicit, explaining that in my culture we tended to discuss the problem — something like (c) above. He adjusted and things went fairly smoothly. In turn, when he was feeling down, I would try to follow his approach.

In your own culture, whom would you approach for help with street directions? Would you alter your choice if you were in a different culture?

- In a comparative experiment in Iran and in England, it was shown that in Iran, 20 per cent of people in the street pointed a foreigner to a place even if that place did not exist; in England this never happened. In the Iranian case, it seems that the need to be helpful (and perhaps also the avoidance of saying 'I don't know') outweighs the need to be accurate.[24]

NEGOTIATING

The term 'negotiating' can cover a wide range of communication types. We begin, however, with an example of negotiating in its formal political sense.

An analysis of negotiations by the Arab, American and Soviet delegates to the UN Security Council during the 1967 Arab-Israeli War identified three negotiating styles.[25] They are summarised below:

- 'factual-inductive negotiating style': Move from pertinent facts to conclusions. Try to ascertain what the facts are. Find similarities or points which can be discussed with the other party, proceed to formulating conclusions such as a range of action alternatives.

- 'axiomatic-deductive negotiating style': Move from a general principle to particulars which can be easily deduced. The deductions should be easily understandable; clarity is one criterion of proof. It is difficult to move to particulars unless there is agreement on general principles. Compromise has a negative connotation.

- 'intuitive-affective negotiating style': Express positions through appeals and emotions, and linguistic exaggeration. Facts are subordinated to feelings. Intense public outbursts.

Which style belongs to which tribe, at least according to this research study? They are American, Soviet, and Arab, respectively. Of course, you may well ask what nationality the researchers were. (They were American.) Perhaps the descriptions might have been quite different had the research been conducted by analysts from the two other cultures.

How might the different negotiating styles manifest themselves in (and influence) business meetings?

Here is a description of a meeting between Chinese and Australian counterparts on an aid project in China. The Chinese side, prior to the meeting, had been very concerned about the (culturally inappropriate) behaviour of one of the Australians:

> 'The Chinese head-of-project began by praising the work of all people involved in the project. He spoke at length about the difficulties overcome and the enormous contributions made and sacrifices endured by the Australian participants. He enumerated the successes achieved. Only right at the end of the speech did he comment on the importance of careful selection of project members, stressing the importance of respecting others' customs and working for the common good. At no stage was the name of the offending party mentioned, but he expected that from the outset the message was quite clear. Attention to the opening section of the speech would tend to suggest to an Australian that all was well.'[26]

Quite different styles (reflecting different values) can emerge in business negotiations. To take just one example, a refusal to come to the point and discuss the topic of the meeting can frequently signal an inability to agree and the avoidance of a blunt refusal. Is that what it would mean in a business meeting in your tribe?

- One researcher has claimed that the Western negotiating style appears 'aggressive and offensive' to the Japanese. By contrast, 'Japanese rhetoric patterns of interaction tend to express mutuality and the emotive aspects. In fact, "no" almost constitutes a term of abuse in Japanese and equivocation, exiting or even lying is preferred to its use.'[27]

An outright 'no' might, in other words, cause the other person to lose face. It would not be 'polite'.

POLITENESS AND 'FACE'

🖎 All cultures require and value politeness, but the ways in which the politeness is achieved may vary significantly.

If you ask a Thai or Indonesian person how to say 'please' in his language, you will get an answer. If, however, you listen to these people interacting in their cultures on a daily basis, you will hardly ever hear them using this word in daily conversation. What's going on? Are these tribes not very polite? Of course not. They simply have other ways of performing politeness.

- A Chinese person has said: 'Australians are always saying "thank you" — "thank you" for this, "thank you" for that, all sorts of small things. I never remember to say it because really it doesn't mean anything.'[28]

Many speakers of English, when asked to describe politeness, tend to respond by referring to 'thank you' and 'please'. Politeness, of course, is not a matter of using a couple of words. The concept of politeness is one of the most important, but most complex, in communication and we need to look at it in a bit of detail.

Consider the following situation: A businesswoman is visiting another country. While doing some shopping in that country, she notices that the sales staff seldom say anything to her at the end of the transaction (even though language does not appear to be a problem). They merely pass her the change and turn their attention to the next customer. She feels that they are really quite impolite. What could explain this cross-cultural situation?

Cultures differ from one another in a number of ways:

- which situations require politeness;
- who needs to be polite to whom;
- what degree of politeness is necessary; and, most importantly,
- how that politeness is achieved.

But what is politeness? We might say it is showing courtesy, respect and consideration to other people, acknowledging them, and not imposing unnecessarily on them. At a deeper level, we all — and this is surely true in every culture — have two fundamental needs:

(i) We want to be accepted and liked; and

(ii) We want some freedom and control over our actions and not to be constantly impinged on by others.

Communications specialists call these two fundamental needs 'positive face' and 'negative face', respectively.[29] As we will see, they motivate and underlie much of our interaction with people. They form the basis of 'politeness', which specialists analyse as comprising two types: 'positive politeness' and 'negative politeness'. (As you will see, 'politeness' is *not* about the refined niceties of being on our best behaviour for a special occasion. It is the daily grist of communication.)

POSITIVE POLITENESS (ALSO CALLED SOLIDARITY POLITENESS)

In positive politeness, we are addressing the positive face of a person, that is their desire to be accepted. We can do this in many ways, for example by:

- Claiming common ground, using expressions of solidarity ('How's it going, *mate?*');
- Indicating that you might have some understanding of people's preferences and attitudes ('*Don't you think* it's marvellous!');
- Showing people that you feel confident about their ability and willingness to understand you ('I really had a hard time learning to drive, *you know.*').
- Attending to people's needs ('*You must be* hungry. How about some lunch?')

NEGATIVE POLITENESS (ALSO CALLED DEFERENCE POLITENESS)

(Careful: 'negative politeness' doesn't mean impoliteness!)

This kind of strategy is oriented towards people's negative face, that is their desire to maintain their territory and self-determination and not to be imposed on.

Some of the ways we use negative politeness are:

- Avoiding presumptions, by hedging, that is making your intention ambiguous ('I'm *pretty* sure you've got that key.')
- Being pessimistic ('*I don't suppose* you'd like to go to the movies, *would you?*');
- Minimising the imposition ('I *just* wanted to ask you a *small* favour.');
- Showing deference ('*Would you care to* get in the car now, *sir?*');
- Showing that you don't want to impinge on people ('*I know you're very*

busy, but...'; '*I hate to trouble you*, but...');

● Impersonalising yourself and your listener by avoiding any mention of either ('*It appears* that...'), expressing the act as a general rule ('*There's* no running in the hallway.'), or by using impersonalising structures such as the passive in 'Your cooperation *is requested.*'

The issue of 'face' is commonly associated with certain cultures, for example cultures in Asia and the Arab world, and I'm prepared to agree that protecting face is a particularly strong feature in some cultures, but what we have to understand is this:

✍ The concept of 'face' is *universal*. Without it, there would be no politeness.

Let's look at this with an example from Australia, where most people are probably *not* convinced that they are concerned with 'face'. Yet when an Australian woman says to her neighbour, for example, 'Could I have some more coffee please, love' that's exactly what she is doing — protecting her own face and also protecting the face of her listener. This is how we would analyse it:

The woman runs the risk of losing face: her request may be rejected and she herself may be disliked and rejected for being too demanding and pushy. Equally, she may cause the neighbour to lose face: the neighbour may feel that she is given no choice in the matter and is being ordered about. In technical terms, the woman's positive face is under threat and the neighbour's negative face is under threat.

To minimise these risks, the woman chooses an indirect strategy ('could I'): it is not a direct strategy, for example 'give me some more coffee'. The neighbour is given an option, to comply with or refuse the request. Her freedom of choice is intact. She also chooses to express solidarity with her neighbour by using a form of intimacy, 'love' — we are friendly members of the same 'in-group'. She also adds 'please', a standard expression of deference politeness (think of the traditional full version, 'if it pleases you').

In simple terms, the woman is being polite. In more technical terms, she has used solidarity and deference strategies to protect their mutual face. The analysis sounds a little too complex and serious, I know — but it works, right across a wide range of communication and can help us to understand why things break down, particularly interculturally.

How, in general, do we get people to do things? Also, how do we make comments, invite, offer, make suggestions, express opinions, request successfully? How do we negotiate all this?

To answer these questions, we need to understand the range of general

WHAT ARE YOU TRYING TO SAY?

strategies from which cultures select. In general, every time we attempt to achieve something in our communication, we have a range of choices. Here are the main options,[30] each with its pros and cons:

1. We can *avoid* the communicative act entirely.
   This way there are no risks involved and no face is lost; nor, of course, is anything achieved.

2. We can do it *indirectly* (the technical term is 'off record'). For example, we can give a hint, 'It's a bit stuffy in here'; give association clues, 'There's a market tomorrow'; be ironic, 'You're a big help'.
   The potential benefits of going 'off record' are that we might get credit for being tactful and non-coercive; we can avoid responsibility from face damage; and we can give people an opportunity to be seen to care for us (and thus we can test their feelings towards us). On the other hand, the strategy might not succeed, or we might be seen as being devious.

3. We can do it *directly* (the technical term is that we do it 'baldly on-record'). For example, 'Open the window'.
   The potential advantage of this strategy is that it is efficient and unlikely to be misunderstood. You can get credit for honesty, and for indicating that you trust people. On the negative side, people may feel that no solidarity has been expressed or that there has been insufficient deference. They have no way out.

4. We can do it *directly, but take some 'softening action'*, that is we can do something to lessen the risk of face loss, either by using positive or negative politeness. For example, 'Could you open the window?'
   Clearly the advantages are that you have the opportunity to give face through positive or negative politeness. Also, there is a reasonable chance of being understood, although there is a risk that the attempts at solidarity or deference will be rejected.

Note that none of these strategies is inherently more *appropriate* than the others — it will very much depend on the context.

Are there any of the four alternatives above which your tribe would never use under any circumstances? (It strikes me as unlikely.)

- When I discuss this with Australian friends, they often claim that they are very direct — 'We Australians call a spade a spade', as one person put it. Yet when I ask them how, for example, they would ask a secretary to work late, their suggestions are in fact either off-record or severely softened with solidarity and deference, anything but baldly direct. Or when I ask them what they do when they dislike the food a host has prepared for them, suddenly 'the spade' starts changing shape.

Why don't you try identifying which strategies (1, 2, 3, 4 above) are used in the following. If you select number 4, try to determine whether solidarity or deference politeness is being used. Of course, an accurate assessment needs more information about the context in each case, but it should be possible to speculate on the type of strategy being used.

- (writing down a name being spelled over the phone)
  I can't write that fast.

The strategy is off-record (2). A bald on-record strategy would be something like 'Speak more slowly'. Note that going off-record *doesn't* necessarily make the communication softer or more 'polite'. I think I might be offended if someone said this to me, especially if it was someone I didn't know. Of course tone of voice would also be important.

- *Got any coffee?*

This is an off-record strategy (2), used in place of the bald alternative 'Give me some coffee'. Strategies like this have become so conventionalised that they are really almost on-record. I can't comment on whether it is appropriate and polite — that would depend on the circumstances and relationships involved.

- *Have you considered our offer?*

This might be a bald on-record strategy to ask for information, i.e. 'Have you considered it or not'? More likely, it is an off-record (2) way of saying 'What is your response to our offer?'

- *Come here.*

Bald on-record (3).

- *Could you have a look at this if you've got a moment?*

An on-record approach with the conventional softener of 'could' (theoretically, it means something like 'could you do this if you were willing'), and the deference implied by recognising that the other person's time is limited and valuable. (4)

- *What's your name?*

Bald on-record. (3)

- (taking down a customer's details) *And your name was?*

Still on-record but softened by the deference shift to the past tense 'was', perhaps implying that I should know your name already, and I am imposing on you to tell me again. (4)

- *I was really sorry to hear about your grandmother's death.*

Bald on-record (3). A more off-record alternative would be something like 'I heard about your grandmother'.

Native English speakers, be warned. Don't go looking for the same frequency of 'please' and 'thank you' in other tribes and don't jump to any conclusions about politeness if you feel that they are missing. For example, I would never use the Thai word for 'please' in casual conversation — you tend to hear it only in formal speech or in writing. It's simply not the way that Thais are polite to each other and protect each other's face when they speak.

- One common strategy in Thailand is to use the word 'request' — as in '(I) request another coffee'; or the word 'help' — as in 'Help clean the table' (i.e. 'Could you clean the table, please').

- The other standard strategy is to use a range of words at the end of utterances. These so-called 'particles' directly express respect, or encourage compliance and agreement, or communicate solidarity.

Thus taken together, you might hear a Thai customer in a restaurant say something like:

'Help clean table [*encourage*] [*respect*] and request another coffee [*encourage*] [*affection*].'

All this is equivalent to the English: 'Could you clean the table please and can I have another coffee please'. Full of solidarity and deference politeness, but without 'please' and, incidentally, without any personal pronouns (I/you). Rather different to the English, isn't it? But every bit as polite. Yet I have seen English speakers feel frustrated at the lack of the 'please' strategy in Thai, and, conversely, Thai speakers feel frustrated at not having access to particles when speaking English. More seriously, they may make unjustified conclusions about each other's level of politeness.

What linguistic means does the English language have available for expressing politeness in this situation? We can do it baldly on-record ('Clean the table'), go completely off-record ('This table is rather dirty') or soften an on-record strategy ('Would you mind cleaning the table please'), to name just a few of the options. Of course, your tone of voice, your facial expression, and your intonation are also important indicators of politeness.

- ✗ All cultures express politeness by using words like 'please' and 'thank you'.
- ✓ All cultures have standards for politeness and ways of being polite.
- ✗ Westerners aren't concerned about face.
- ✓ All cultures are concerned about face. This is what motivates politeness.
- ✗ Some cultures are more polite than others.
- ✓ There is no objective measure of politeness.

Let's now return to the situation of the businesswoman we saw on p.82. Perhaps it is simply the case that the sales assistants' culture has 'decided' that service interactions of this kind require only a very low degree of politeness — while perhaps their standard in *other* situations is to express a degree of politeness that the businesswoman would find quite effusive.

Alternatively, perhaps the politeness was expressed in a way that the businesswoman simply failed to notice, because she was expecting a version of her own culture's requirement (perhaps a phrase such as 'Thank you very much'). It is possible that the sales staff smiled at her or nodded their heads slightly. Remember the example of Chinese people in restaurants thanking waiters by unobtrusively tapping the table with their fingers.

In our own culture, we usually 'perform' politeness quite unthinkingly: it is 'programmed' into our behaviour. We tend to become aware of politeness only when (i) we feel somebody within our culture has ignored or forgotten the requirement, or (ii) in cross-cultural situations, where we encounter a strategy which is unfamiliar to our standards (as in the example of the businesswoman, above).

The choice of politeness strategies depends on at least three cultural variables:

1. (perception of) social distance
2. (perception of) the relative power
3. (perception of) the imposition involved.

In your culture, how would you behave and what would you say to indicate various degrees of politeness in the following situations?

- Stopping somebody on the street to ask for directions.
- Declining an invitation to a party.
- Asking a colleague for help at work.
- Introducing a colleague to your family.
- Arriving in class late.

Having decided for your own culture, analyse them against the five options. Now imagine how these same 'acts' might be carried out politely in other cultures.

Consider the following examples from English, still with our conference group. In both examples, the participants correctly interpret the strategies and respond appropriately. Do you understand them? Could you respond appropriately?

A: Are you going to finish that last sandwich?
B: Go ahead.

X: Are you going shopping tomorrow after the conference?
Y: Is the Pope Catholic?
X: (*laughs*) How do you feel about a partner?
Y: Sure. Shall we meet in the lobby?

What strategies are these people using to communicate? You may need to refer back to the four strategies described on p.85. You will see that their strategies are off-record. The bald on-record alternatives might be something like:

A: I want that last sandwich.

B: Go ahead.

X: Are you going shopping tomorrow after the conference?

Y: Yes, I certainly am.

X: I want to come with you.

Y: Sure. Meet me in the lobby.

Cultures may differ as to how frequently they favour either indirect or direct strategies. Having said that, I must admit I don't agree with the conventional view that Western cultures are very direct and Eastern cultures are very indirect. I know this view will be scorned, but I am committed to it nevertheless. For me, the difference is not *global*, i.e. that one culture is *inherently* more indirect than another culture. Rather, the differences come in:

- whether they will tend to choose either a direct or indirect strategy in a particular situation or on a particular topic; and
- how they achieve their indirect strategies.

Naturally, these differences can cause difficulties in intercultural communication.

But first, here is an amusing example from the U.S.A.[31] In this extract, three authors write to their publisher, asking for their checks:

From Sid Silverman
$ $ $ $ $ $ $ $ $ $ $ $ $ $?????????????!!!!!!!!!!!!

From Vince Vitucci
Look, I've got to have my check right away. I've got kids to feed.

From Florence King
Isn't it terrible how careless the post office is getting these days? So much mail is delayed or even lost that I have been concerned whether I have missed any recent letters from you. I do feel quite sure, however, that once again the blame should be cast on the government and not on you, for I know how prompt you are about answering your mail and keeping abreast of even the most minor details. I shall look forward to hearing from you in the very near future.

Guess who was the last to get paid?

What strategies did the three letter-writers use? Clearly, the first two are very different versions of a 'bald' on-record approach, while the third is very 'off-record' with a lot of positive and negative politeness.

More seriously, the role of politeness strategies in presentation of self (see page 77) can have critical consequences:

- One study examined cultural differences in the interaction of Alaska Natives with the American legal system, particularly with regard to the preparation of pre-sentence reports. The research showed that the Alaska Natives show a strong preference for *deference* politeness (be pessimistic and do not make any claims about future improvements or future hopes, all of which sounds like an admission of guilt), whereas the court expects *solidarity* politeness (be optimistic, show group membership by aligning yourselves with other members of society, put your best foot forward, all of which is interpreted as respect for the law).[32]

At Korean President Kim Young-sam's first televised news conference a Korean reporter asked who might succeed him in five years. Mr Kim's eyes twinkled. He smiled, leaned towards the lectern and said: 'Koreans are too impatient.' Everyone, including Mr Kim, laughed.[33]

Clearly the members of this tribe understand Mr Kim's 'off-record' reply. They share the same background knowledge, values, and expectations so that they can decode the intention. In other words, this is 'high-context' communication, where speakers and listeners rely on a shared context. In contrast, low-context communication does not rely on a shared context of knowledge and understanding; it is explicit and unambiguous ('on-record'). In the Korean example, what would a *low*-context response be?

Are the following types of communication usually 'high' or 'low' in context?

1. business contracts
2. legal proceedings
3. traditional dance forms
4. abstract art
5. news broadcasts
6. conversations between close friends
7. conversations between acquaintances
8. jokes

Clearly, 1 and 2 will usually be very *low*-context, as should 5, though to a lesser extent. In turn, we would expect 7 to require a lower level of shared context than 6. In contrast, 3, 4, and 8 will tend to be high context.

Reliance on context may differ from culture to culture.

- 'The Japanese think intelligent beings should be able to discover the point of a discourse from the context, which they are careful to provide. The Japanese see our syllogistic method and its deductive reasoning as an effort to get inside their heads and do their thinking for them.'[34]

Of course all cultures use both high-context and low-context communication. Here again is a light-hearted example from an American author. In this extract she has just had a story published in a magazine:

> When the complimentary copy arrived I showed it to Granny. Immensely pleased, she gazed at the name for several minutes and then adjusted her bifocals and began reading the story. Suddenly her smile faded and she handed the magazine back to me. 'Your grandfather was a perfect gentleman.'[35]

In this extract, the cultural high context is further enhanced by the high context of a close long-term relationship between the two people involved.

The issue of context is relevant also in presenting your ideas.

PRESENTING IDEAS

A German book, hailed as a landmark in its field by German reviewers, was described, when it was published in an English translation, as 'chaotic' and criticised for its 'lack of focus and cohesiveness', 'haphazardness of presentation' and 'poor organisation'.[36] How is this possible?

Research indicates that German academic writing favours 'parenthetical amplifications of subordinate elements', that is, taking side-tracks to expand on relatively minor points, before picking up the main thread again. Even in the conclusion, there might be digressions. This style of presentation is not well regarded in the English-speaking academic world (as many foreign students studying at English-speaking universities have found).

Another style of presenting information is found in Japanese. Here, one of the characteristic patterns of speeches and written work is to provide a series of points — a bit like stepping stones in a stream. The reader or listener is expected to provide the jumps in between — and draw the conclusions.

Here is yet another instance of different cultural expectations in presenting information and ideas.

> 'An Australian adviser involved in formulating policy on the future of Chinese students in Australia at the time of the Tianamen massacre asked a prominent Chinese intellectual for his opinion. The intellectual replied by summarising the experience of the Chinese students, explaining their motives for coming to Australia in the first place and the impact on their thinking both of events in China and the uncertainty of Australian government policy. The summary was an intelligent and carefully reasoned analysis of the situation and finished with a number of clearly stated proposals. The adviser, however, was wearing a faintly glazed expression by the end of the talk and later commented that he had had difficulty in picking up the

thread of the argument being presented. He felt that the intellectual had not really thought out his case and that his ideas were vague and unorganised.'[37]

If you have little experience in reading texts outside your culture, I urge you to read, in full, the text below. It was written by a Korean scholar and was published in the English language newspaper, the *Korean Times*.[38]

If you had any difficulty in following this text, what are the possible sources of that difficulty?

- Perhaps it is because of the relatively high context — that is, the writer assumes that his readers share the background knowledge of the issues under examination (but as an outsider you don't).

- Perhaps, also, it is because the information and ideas are presented in ways that don't conform with your expectations. You may feel he

It has been reported that the Ministry of Home Affairs is planning to lengthen the period of training for public officials from the present 3 days to 6 days per annum in order to solidify their spiritual stance and probably at the [Spiritual Cultural Institute] which is normally and aptly translated as the Institute for Korean Studies. Here the term [spiritual] has the additional meaning 'national' in addition to its conventional meanings as incorporeal, moral, intellectual, etc.

Though I doubt that this new meaning will take root in the English language the semantic distortion of the original Korean word… may establish itself in the Korean language some day as we see in the widely accepted tautological compound [spiritual culture]. I would accept this term if there were such a thing as material culture. I suspect that the term was coined originally by pedantic nationalists.

Some years ago I heard a member of the Korean Alphabet Society complain that the architectural design and the internal decoration of the Institute for Korean Studies made it resemble a Buddhist temple, which he did not regard as traditionally Korean. His question was: 'Are all these Chinese characters spiritually tenable?' The questioner apparently regarded the Institute as a place for enhancing the Korean spirit as it was intended to be. However, many Korean people would no doubt regard Buddhism as a traditionally Korean religion though it was imported from India. How should we interpret the historically attested strong national movements on the part of the Korean Christians? Is Christianity less Korean than Buddhism because of its short history in this nation? Note also that all those Sino-Korean words which comprise more than 50 per cent of the total lexical entries in Korean language dictionaries are no longer regarded as foreign words.

It is then not difficult to see that any attempt to demarcate what is national and what is foreign is doomed to fail in most instances, and that such an attempt is often unworthy and unnecessary, if not trivial.

I do not, however, advocate anarchism or antinationalism. I am well aware that the geopolitical characteristics of this country requires some nationalist stance for security reasons. All I want 'doesn't get to the point' or that he includes 'irrelevant' detail. Of course, 'relevant' is as slippery a concept as 'good' or 'polite'; in other words, it very much depends on your (cultural) point of view.

- Perhaps the organisation of ideas causes you difficulty, particularly his reserving the main point till the very end. (English writing tends to present the main point first and then support this idea.)

If you were a newspaper editor in your tribe, what changes might you make to this text? Alternatively, if the writer of this text were a postgraduate student under your supervision, would you require any changes in his approach to structuring and presenting information?

More broadly what are the implications for international education? If this Korean writer were your student, it is important to understand that he has not failed to fulfil standards of scholarly writing. Rather, he has his *own* standards for

to point out is that too much emphasis on nationalism may do more harm than good to the nation.

Therefore, instead of inspiring nationalism we should appeal to universal reason and proper moral conduct which clearly take precedence over parochial nationalism. The erection of the Independence Memorial Hall will hopefully enhance the patriotic spirit, but in case the patriotic spirit can not trigger the civil spirit, love of one's immediate neighbour, it will mean very little, for the civil spirit must take precedence over the national spirit, though the relationship between the two is certainly reciprocal.

I am constantly reminded of this simple truth whenever I change my subway at Sinsoldong interchange. Despite the loudspeaker's warning against passengers'

trespassing on the security line, many of them rush into the cars en masse to occupy seats for themselves for the less than 15-minute ride to the Chamil sports complex terminal, where the 1988 Olympics are to be held. I wonder how we enhance the nation's prestige through a sports event. To make the funny sight funnier, this often happens even when there are not enough passengers to fill the seats available! I don't want to blame anybody but myself because as a career teacher I am partly responsible for this deplorable situation. What a moral degeneration! As a middle-school boy I never dreamed of taking a seat in a long distance bus which carried me for two days from one end of Hwanghae Province to the other.

Spiritual poverty or the lack of civil spirit may best

be observed in a metropolitan area like Seoul. I really do not understand why our public transit system is so multi-layered. At the bottom there are cheap buses which are sophistically called 'standing seats'... buses which provide very few seats. The regular buses with seats, charging three times the fare for a standing seat bus. Finally taxis which move about constantly to catch more passengers.

Once you get on one of these you have to listen to whatever pops out of the radio at the mercy of the fingertip of the driver who seems to be deaf to any big noise.

Dear administrators, please do not talk about spiritual things unless you are interested in implementing concrete ethical conduct.

what is appropriate and effective. To judge this writing against your own expectations would be totally ethnocentric. (On the other hand, there may, of course, be a reasonable expectation for him to learn and adjust to your 'rules' if he is studying in your country).

🖉 Even allowing for individual differences, cultures tend to use standard ways of structuring and presenting information. These ways differ across cultures.

In this chapter we have only been able to give a very brief overview of communication. At the very least, I hope it is clear that communication is multi-factorial and multi-dimensional.

OBSERVATION CHECKLIST

These are just some of the aspects of communication you may need to keep an eye on interculturally:

- body language
- address systems
- openings and closings
- topic choice
- turn control
- quantity of talk
- style of talk
- paying attention

- apologising
- complimenting
- self-presentation
- helping and advising
- politeness and 'face'
- negotiating
- advising and helping
- presenting information

ACTION LIST

🖉 Accept that all cultures — even your own — impose some constraints on the body.

🖉 Remember that different rules about appropriate use of the body can lead to intercultural misunderstandings.

🖉 Keep asking for advice about what to call people. There will generally be somebody who can get you started in the right direction.

🖉 Don't automatically follow the address systems you hear. The people of the tribe might not find it appropriate to integrate you into their systems.

🖉 Don't take offence when somebody gets the form of address 'wrong' — it is rarely intended to be offensive.

🖉 Remember that how people open and close their conversations will differ culturally.

🖉 Understand that cultures don't necessarily choose the same topics to talk about.

🖉 Remember that all cultures have some topics they would rather avoid.

- Observe how other cultures join in and take turns in a conversation. The rules will probably be different from your own.
- Remember that, even allowing for individual differences, each culture probably has a distinctive 'communicative style'.
- Take care: your way of showing that you are paying attention may be considered inappropriate by other cultures.
- Remember that all functions of communication (whether complimenting, apologising, requesting, inviting, or offering) proceed according to different cultural rules.
- Understand that cultures have different goals in 'self-presentation' — that is, in the positive qualities about themselves they strive to present.
- Understand, also, that even if cultures have the same self-presentation goals, their ways of achieving these may differ.
- Accept that all cultures require and value politeness, but the ways in which the politeness is achieved may vary significantly.
- Remember that the concept of 'face' is *universal*. Without it, there would be no politeness.
- Don't make the mistake of assuming that all cultures express politeness by using words like 'please' and 'thank you'.
- Try to eliminate the idea that some cultures are more polite than others.
- Remember that there is no objective measure of politeness.
- Remember that, even allowing for individual differences, cultures tend to use standard ways of structuring and presenting information. These ways differ across cultures.

Given the complexity of communication, how can we manage interculturally?

'Pleased to meet you.'

Developing the right skills
Managing intercultural communication

4

IN previous chapters we've seen the impact of culture on our being, seeing, behaving, and communicating. At the same time, however, we are not of course the mindless products of cultural programming — *we are in control of our communication.* We have a number of skills to enable us to *manage* communication.

Before we look at the issue of managing intercultural communication, let's first recap our general approach. How do you feel about these principles?

- ✍ It is seldom necessary to *change* your culture, although some modifications may be practical at times.

- ✍ It is not necessary to *like* the culture(s) we engage with — that's probably not realistic — but a degree of respect is essential.

- ✍ It is not necessarily our aim to *accept* other cultures, but it is essential to accept that other cultures are valid (at least for their members).

- ✍ It is not necessarily our aim to *understand* everything about the cultures we engage with — a very difficult task for an outsider. Instead, we need to understand that culture influences people's perceptions, behaviour, value systems and ways of communicating, and we need to try to determine which characteristics of a particular culture are the critical ones.

- ✍ Our aim is not to become more sensitive, open-minded people (although this would not be a bad outcome); our aim is to become more *skilled.*

How much *effort* should we put into intercultural communication? How hard, for example, should we seek to analyse behaviour and how many adjustments should we make? In no way am I suggesting that we need to monitor everything and adjust to everything — that would be both impractical and totally unnecessary.

Instead, our actions will depend on several factors:[1]

- On whose territory does the contact occur?
- What is the time span of the interaction?
- What is the purpose of the interaction?
- How frequent are the contacts?
- What is the degree of intimacy, relative status and power, and numerical balance of the participants?
- What is the relative cost/benefit of making an effort to manage the interaction successfully?

One or more of these factors will determine how much effort we put into a particular instance of intercultural communication.

What's involved in successful intercultural communication? As with many human endeavours, there are three components: *knowledge, awareness,* and *skill.*

Knowledge, awareness, and skill: to be successful in intercultural communication, you can do without one of these. Which one?

I would suggest that it is 'knowledge'. Knowledge of how other cultures work is never irrelevant or useless — as long as it's accurate knowledge. Indeed, in long-term or permanent intercultural situations (such as foreign study, overseas postings, or migration), knowledge is very important at a practical level. Facing a job interview, writing a paper for a university course, undertaking difficult business negotiations, are all challenging when performed interculturally. *But* there are limits to knowledge. We can't, and don't need to, know everything.

> 'It is often said that those who visit China for a week write a book about it. Those who stay a month write an article. And those who live here a year or more — write nothing.'[2]

On the other hand, nor do we want to have too small a base of knowledge about a culture. There are dangers in reducing the complexity of a culture to a list of do's and don'ts. This is the approach common in guide books. It's not that these guides give inaccurate information — although that does happen quite often unfortunately. The bigger problem tends to be that everything is presented as a simplified 'fact' — with no insight behind it, and no possibility of diversity or complexity. Also, which 'facts' have they selected, and why these particular facts? If the naïve reader assumes that 'learning the list' leads to successful intercultural communication, there could be some unpleasant experiences!

The critical requirement in successful intercultural communication is *not* knowledge of cultures — no matter how desirable that may be — but, rather, awareness or attitude.

AWARENESS (ATTITUDE)

Throughout this book I have argued for the following points of awareness and attitude:

- be aware of the nature and significance of culture
- realise the impact of culture on communication
- be willing to acknowledge the existence and validity of other ways of being, seeing, doing, and communicating

It all comes down to this. It's fair to assume that people always have a purpose behind their behaviour and their communication. They know what they are doing, they know what they want to achieve, how they want to present themselves to other people, and what response they expect from other people.

Even if their communication and behaviour seem strange, unclear, unsuccessful or unacceptable to us, we can be certain that it makes sense and is acceptable to them. In technical terms, they are 'rational agents'.

Without acceptance of this point, it is difficult to imagine developing intercultural skills.

SKILLS

Here are the aims in intercultural communication:

- to be able to *avoid* miscommunication which is due to cultural factors
- to be able to *recognise* when miscommunication could be due to cultural factors
- to be able to *repair* miscommunication which may be due to cultural factors

Different kinds of skills, each with specific strategies, are needed if these aims are to be met, and we will look at each of them in turn:

- externalisation skills
- monitoring skills
- communication skills
- anxiety management skills
- tactical skills
- investigative skills

When written in a list like this, the skills may sound rather daunting, but they aren't really. Most of them are skills we use in our daily interactions, even within our own culture.

EXTERNALISATION SKILLS: STEPPING OUTSIDE YOUR USUAL PERCEPTIONS

'Externalising' simply means stepping outside yourself and seeing yourself, your behaviour, and your communication from an outsider's perspective.

This, of course, is what we have been doing throughout this book — stepping outside our own (culture's) behaviours, perceptions, assumptions, values, and communication — which we believe to be normal, natural and appropriate — and seeing that (i) alternative norms are possible, and (ii) alternative perceptions of *our* norms are possible.

- Let's call this 'normal' mode — or to use a computer analogy, our 'default' mode — our ALPHA mode. It is the way we are, making automatic assumptions and interpretations based on our own culture.
- People are capable, however, of seeing alternatives or speculating about alternatives. We will call this (externalised) mode the BETA mode.
- Finally, people are also able to identify when their base assumptions, perceptions, behaviours, and communication do not appear to be

functioning as they normally would. They cannot, however, see a viable alternative. We will call this our X mode. In other words: 'I don't know.'

Let's apply the analysis to the following example, where you are interpreting someone's communication. What interpretation would you form if you were the worker in this office situation?

Boss: That's about it, I think. So... I hope you enjoy working here. And remember: if you have any problems, don't hesitate to ask me.

Worker: —

What is your ALPHA interpretation of what this boss has said? Is it one of the following?

● He's just giving a general assurance that he is willing to help. He probably says that to all new staff.

● It sounds like he suspects I'm going to have problems or maybe even to cause problems. It's a warning.

● He's telling me I must come and see him when I have problems. It's an instruction.

Can you see any alternative (BETA) interpretations? (If not, you will have to agree that you are in X mode.)

Consider the following situations. Again, decide your ALPHA mode, try to find BETA alternatives — or if this fails — declare that you don't know (X mode). In the analysis under each example, I have taken the ALPHA response from my own tribe and the BETA responses from a range of various cultures with which I am familiar.

● A man gets into a taxi. Where does he sit?

ALPHA: Traditionally, in the front next to the driver. Nowadays, maybe in the back, maybe in the front.
BETA: In the back, of course.

● You receive a gift from colleagues in your office. You have the gift in your hands. What do you do next?

ALPHA: Open it and thank them.
BETA: Thank them and open it later.

● The guests at a dinner eat with loud sucking noises.

ALPHA: They're rather impolite and inconsiderate.
BETA: They're showing their enjoyment of the food in a perfectly normal manner.

- When a woman marries, does her name change?
  - ALPHA: It's up to her.
  - BETA: Yes, of course.

- While teaching a class, your teacher sits on the desk in the front of the room. What do you think of his behaviour?
  - ALPHA: Nothing.
  - BETA: He's very impolite.

- You are sitting with a group of colleagues on your living room floor (examining some documents, say). To make your guests more comfortable, you pass each of them a cushion. They do not sit on the cushions. Instead, they hug the cushions for the rest of the evening. Why do they do that?
  - ALPHA: —
  - BETA: Since cushions are intended for the head, and the head is sacred, you shouldn't put your backside on them.
  - X: I have no idea.

- You are in a restaurant and you want to call a waiter. How do you do it?
  - ALPHA: 'Excuse me.'
  - BETA: 'Older brother.'

- A man has lit your cigarette for you and you want to thank him. What do you do?
  - ALPHA: Say 'thanks.'
  - BETA: Tap his hand.

- You are eating in a restaurant with a group of colleagues and the bill arrives. What do you do next?
  - ALPHA: It depends. Maybe I'll offer to pay, but more likely we'll calculate the shared cost.
  - BETA: Insist that I pay.

- Your host has given you a cup of tea. What do you do next?
  - ALPHA: Thank him and start drinking the tea.
  - BETA: Wait till he invites me to drink it.

- You are eating your lunch, sitting on a bench in the park, when a colleague comes up to you. What do you do next?
  - ALPHA: Chat to him.
  - BETA: Offer him some of my lunch.

- You meet an acquaintance on the street. The first thing she says to you is 'Where are you going?' What does she mean by this question?

  ALPHA: She wants to know where I'm going.
  BETA: She's greeting me.

- Your first impressions, your 'gut reactions' are probably right.
- Your first impressions, your 'gut reactions' are probably highly ethnocentric. Go for a second reaction instead.

How would you describe the following events in your culture? Suppose you are talking to a 'Martian' who has come to observe your tribe. (You might look back to the outsider's description of the wedding on page 7 to help you get the right 'objective' distance from something you take for granted):

- a funeral
- a business meeting
- a family breakfast

Then try the following dialogue. If you were Wai in this situation, what would be your first instinctive interpretation of the communication and then — on reflection — what might be another possible interpretation? Then do the same for Speaker Eks.

Eks: And your wife, Mr Wai?
Wai: Actually, I'm divorced.
Eks: Oh, what a pity. What happened?

Let us assume for the moment that Mr Wai's culture has quite strong constraints on such a question. If he remains in his ALPHA mode, he might move straight to a response like 'That's none of your business!'

Realising, however, that he is communicating interculturally, Mr. Wai could instead consider alternative explanations. Can you see alternatives?

  BETA: Perhaps it is acceptable to discuss such matters in his culture. Maybe he's just wanting to show concern or empathy. He probably doesn't want me to actually give him an account of my marriage and divorce. Maybe it's a formula — just like when I ask someone 'How are you?' — I certainly don't expect them to actually give me a medical account. Also, presumably, he's not trying to be rude.

Wai is on his way to repairing the situation.

Of course Eks has also gone for an ALPHA behaviour, in assuming that this topic and his approach to the topic are universally accepted.

Consider the following situation. Note what your ALPHA response would be, and then shift immediately to an alternative BETA explanation. If you can't, move to the X mode ('I don't know'). Remember: Moving to the X mode is often a better idea than always being stuck in your ALPHA mode.

● You're a teacher. One of your students brings an assignment to you late. She apologises very politely and then giggles, covering her mouth.

Of course, we can use the same ALPHA/BETA/X analysis to consider not only the interpretation of other people's communication, but also in *initiating* our own communication.

Take the following simple example. You are going to meet the chief executive officer of a company with whom you are opening negotiations. You have not met her before and you know nothing about her culture.

ALPHA: I will greet her in the only way I know how (for example, shake hands, smile, and say 'how do you do').

BETA: I realise of course that her style of greeting may be quite different from mine. Maybe she prefers not to shake hands.

X: I really don't know what is best. I'll try to find out if I get the chance.

Note that externalisation doesn't threaten your own culture. You can step right back into your own shoes when you have finished!

Here are some more tasks that should give you a feel for externalisation:

● First, answer this question: In your culture, do elderly people (a) tend to live with their adult children or relatives, or (b) tend to live independently or in retirement homes?

● Did you answer (a) or (b)? Now, imagine that the opposite were true (that is, swap 'shoes') and answer one of the following sets of questions.

(a) Remember: Answer these questions if *in fact* elderly people tend to live with their families in your culture.

Why does your culture put its elderly people in retirement homes? Don't you love them? Don't you respect them any more? Aren't they upset to be abandoned by their families?

(b) Remember: Answer these questions if *in fact* elderly people tend to live independently or in retirement homes in your culture.

Why do elderly people in your culture live with their families? Is it because they want to or isn't there any economic alternative? Do the elderly people still try to control their adult children's lives? How can you have any privacy?

It's quite difficult, isn't it? Remember you don't have to agree with or believe in what you're saying (your shoes are waiting comfortably for you back in your own culture), but it is useful to be able to understand a different perspective.

If, in this task, you find that you really can't explain a cultural 'position', then you have difficulty in externalising.

When you complete the task, you might like to try the same approach in the following hypothetical situations. Decide which of the alternatives in the following pairs appropriately describes you, then 'swap' and describe what it is like (or why you hold that belief):

- I'm male. / I'm female.
- I believe in arranged marriages. / I believe in people selecting their own marriage partners.
- I believe that children should obey their parents in all respects. / I believe that children have the right, on occasion, to question their parents' instructions.
- I'm a Muslim. / I have a different religion (or no religion at all).

Again, if you find this impossibly difficult — or if you refuse even to contemplate the alternative! — then intercultural awareness may be difficult for you. You may nevertheless still be able to develop a considerable degree of skill in intercultural communication. If you find that you are able, to some extent, at least, to see the world in a different way, or to 'be' someone else (even if it is temporary only), then a very considerable degree of intercultural skill is within your reach. Also, if you found yourself saying, 'Well, I don't really know. I wonder what/why...', this is great. You are in X-mode, and on your way to better intercultural communication.

OK, let's go back to our own comfortable shoes.

ANALYTICAL SKILLS: FIGURING OUT WHAT'S GOING ON

A prerequisite for developing our analytic skills is that we have externalisation skills.

Here our aim is to spot the 'problem' (or potential problem) in communication situations, and analyse the possible source of those problems.

Generally speaking, you may find that the problem is one of:

- language
- conflicting communication styles and strategies
- conflicting cultural values or assumptions (the 'ALPHAS' don't match)

I've given 15 examples below for us to look at and analyse. Try to analyse each of the samples yourself, before you look at my interpretations.

1. *A:* Hi. How are you? I haven't seen you for months.

    B: Yeah. I've been working overseas.

    A: Oh, I see. (*smiling*) Gee, you look so fat!

    B: Oh... I... Um...

A: Look at your cheeks — (*laughing*) so fat!

B: (*puzzled and irritated*) Well, yes. I suppose I...

Analysis: There appear to be no language problems here, but some mismatch of values and expectations appears to occur. Culture A presumably values weight as an indicator of good health, robustness, and perhaps even prosperity — and may express this 'compliment' even if the other party shows no sign of physical change at all. That is, it may be figuratively rather than literally intended. (Compare the English expression in this situation: 'You're looking well', often used formulaically rather than literally).

Speaker B, on the other hand, does not share this concept or 'formula' and seems to have interpreted it literally. In A's culture, an increase in weight may be regarded as unattractive or a sign of lack of self-discipline.

Cultures A and B may share the same goal (i.e. try to say something pleasant and positive to someone you haven't seen in quite a while), but have different ways of achieving this shared goal (i.e. comment on the person's weight versus comment on the person's health).

Repair: Speaker B should not trust her first assumption, namely that a statement of weight gain is intended literally. If she feels concerned about A's statement, she should attempt a direct repair such as, 'Sorry, but people in my culture get a bit upset when you tell them they're fat.' Speaker A, in turn, should not assume that her formula will transfer successfully into another culture. To repair the problem she could ask Speaker B (or someone else) why her statement has drawn this reaction.

2. This situation presents the perspectives of three people: (A) a supervisor showing a new staff member around on his first day, (B) the staff member himself, and (C) another worker who observed all of the above.

A: The new guy started today. I took him around and introduced him to everyone in the section. He looked pretty shy and uncomfortable, which surprised me a bit because the staff were really friendly to him. Then I sat him down at his desk and talked through his responsibilities with him. I really don't know if he understood, but he said he did. Well, we'll see. He seems pretty bright, but I don't think he's got much initiative.

B: I started work today. The supervisor took me around and introduced me to everyone in the section. They weren't very friendly, but I didn't let them see how uncomfortable that made me feel. Then we went to the supervisor's desk and he talked about the company. It was very interesting and I really paid attention, although he really doesn't speak very clearly. I think I made a good impression on him. I suppose my briefing will start tomorrow.

C. The new guy started work today. The supervisor took him around and introduced him to everyone in the section. He seemed really relaxed and friendly, and everyone seemed to get on well with him. Then they went to his new desk and the supervisor explained all the regulations to him. He did it really well, but I don't think the new guy was paying much attention. I don't think the supervisor was too impressed. He seems like a friendly guy, though — always smiling.

Analysis: The problem stems from different *communicative styles*. Clearly, all three participants are in ALPHA mode. It is their first instinctive interpretations which they form and retain without questioning. There is no attempt to externalise, to consider alternative (that is, 'BETA'-type) interpretations, or of suspending judgement until they have more information, that is leaving issues open: posing questions, rather than coming to conclusions.

More specifically, there are differences in 'attending' behaviour and expectations.

I really paid attention. (*Speaker B*)
I don't think the new guy was paying much attention. (*Speaker C*)

Perhaps the third person's culture uses more overt verbalisations to indicate attention, while the second speaker's culture uses, say, fixed body position and averted eyes to indicate polite attention.

There are also differences in interpreting the purpose of communication, perhaps due to unsuccessful off-record strategies.

I talked through his responsibilities with him. (*Speaker A*)
He talked about the company... I suppose my briefing will start tomorrow. (*Speaker B*)

There are also differences in interpretation of emotion and attitude, as expressed through body language and expectations of behaviours, and perhaps topic choice and off-record strategies:

The staff were really friendly to him. (*Speaker A*)
They weren't very friendly (to me).(*Speaker B*)
Everyone seemed to get on well with him.(*Speaker C*)

Repair: Far more useful for each of the speakers would be an 'X' strategy of the 'I don't know for sure what's going on here/I wonder what's going on here' type. This seems particularly important for Speakers A and B, who both need to be more explicit and to clarify each other's communication (see pages 122–29).

3. *A:* Did you enjoy the book?
   B: Of course.
   A: (*looks taken aback*)

Analysis: The problem here is probably *language*, rather than one of different values. Presumably, B has selected this routine, intending it to have the meaning 'Yes, I sure/really did'. (The equivalent to 'of course' is used this way in quite a number of languages, actually.) A's ALPHA response, however is to interpret it to mean: 'What a silly question'.

Repair: A could remember that there is probably a good reason why B has responded this way — even if he doesn't know what it is — and should not take offence. B might take note of A's facial expression and ask him (or another person) why his response has caused this reaction.

4. A group of Australian postgraduate Linguistic students were working with a Cameroonian 'informant' (himself a postgraduate student, but in a different field). Their aim was to write an analysis of the informant's language. One day, when after weeks of effort they thought they had finally worked out the system of tones in the language, they tested their hypothesis on the informant, only to discover that it was totally wrong. They burst out laughing. The Cameroonian informant left the room angrily.

Analysis: The problem here has to do with different *communicative styles*: in particular, different functions for (and interpretations of) laughter. The students were directing their laughter at themselves, expressing their frustration at their own incompetence. The Cameroonian assumed the laughter was directed at him and his language.

Repair: This incident actually happened and I had to go to our Cameroonian colleague and do some explicit repair. In retrospect, we might have avoided laughing (if that were possible) or at least been aware of the risk of misinterpretation and immediately explained our behaviour: 'We're laughing at ourselves.' In turn, our colleague should, I suppose, have not moved quite so automatically to his ALPHA interpretation. Laughter can cause all sorts of problems cross-culturally.

5. *A:* That was a great report you gave me. Just what I had in mind.
    B: Oh, no. I didn't think so. There were so many mistakes.
    A: (*puzzled*) Mistakes? No, there weren't.

Analysis: Here we are dealing with *different values*. B's culture presumably values being humble and requires that a person modestly deflect a compliment (rather than, say, thanking the person who has made the compliment). A appears to take the reference to 'mistakes' quite literally.

Repair: A could speculate about the reasons for B's behaviour and, if she has access to resources, do a little 'research' over a period of time. Having come to understand the two different styles, she might in a future similar situation either (a) make an explicit reference to the difference: 'B, now I know you're not going to accept this, but I really think you did a great job on that Exo account', or (b) make no adjustments. In turn, B could, over a period of time, observe how people of A's culture react to compliments. Having ultimately understood the two different styles, she might then in a future similar situation either (a) adjust her own style a little next time, or (b) make an explicit bid to explain and keep her own style: 'A, you know, in my country when someone praises you, we ....', or (c) choose to make no adjustment at all.

6. (In a job interview)

    A: What do you think this company is going to offer you that your present company doesn't offer you?

    B: Well, there are quite a lot of things, for example like, um ... the Christmas bonus.

    A: Um-hm...

    B: So many things, holidays and all that. You get more holidays here.

    A: (*laughs*) Alright... OK.

Analysis: Probably the problem lies in *different values*. In this situation, A's culture may value statements which reflect ambition, initiative, and so on, and is asking this question to give the candidate an opportunity to 'sell' himself. B's culture, on the other hand, may favour a direct and honest answer, indicating why the candidate has decided to apply.

Repair: Job interviews are very difficult interculturally: they often have very different scripts and expectations in different cultures. Although one might say that the interviewer has to broaden his insight and move beyond his ALPHA behaviours, this seldom happens in practice. Realistically, the applicant (who has less power) will probably have to do his homework and investigate the expectations of interviewers in the target culture. Incidentally, this is an authentic example.

7. A: We'll need a minibus to pick them up at the airport. It'll have to seat at least 12 people. And don't forget to contact the hotel people to reconfirm their arrival. Now, the reception starts at 8.00. Have you got that?

    B: Yes.

    A: So we'll have to leave the hotel no later than 7.30. I think we should all assemble in the Takra Room on the second floor. Is that clear?

    B: Yes.

    A: OK. Now the G.M. will have to be there and his wife of course. And I want all the Section heads there too. And they'd better be on time, or heads will roll, believe me. It's really important. Are you listening?

    B: Yes, of course.

    A: Now remember – the chairman's name is Sitompul S-i-t-o-m-p-u-l and the deputy is Prabowo – P-r-a-. Have you got that?

> *B:* Yes
>
> *A:* Hmm. I hope so. Now where was I?. P-r-a-b-o-w-o-

Analysis: Here we encounter *different communicative styles*. It appears that A and B have different approaches to acknowledging complex information/instructions. A seems to be looking for more explicit acknowledgement strategies — perhaps using words like 'Uh-uh', 'Yes, I understand' while listening to the instructions, or perhaps doing partial echoes of the instructions ('Yes. 7.30. I've got that' / 'The Takra room'). B, on the other hand, shows that he is attending by concentrating and listening carefully.

Repair: A could shift his strategy. If he is concerned whether B is attending he could explicitly ask for a recap of the instructions: 'Now, let's just check all that. Could you run through all the details for me, just to see that we're absolutely clear.' B, in turn, perhaps needs to investigate the reason for A's irritation, perhaps by observing other people (from A's culture) listening to instructions.

> 8. *A:* Yes, it's good, but maybe just a bit hard to read. Have you thought about spreading it over two pages?
>
> *B:* No, I haven't.

Analysis: Again, *different communicative styles* are posing the problem. A presumably has chosen this indirect strategy as a way of making a recommendation (or even instruction). B, on the other hand, has interpreted it as a (direct) information question.

Repair: Both A and B need to speculate about and, if possible, research the source of their problem. Having done this, A might choose a more direct strategy in the future: 'I think you should spread this over two...' B could in future use an overt 'checking' strategy, if he is not certain of A's intent: 'Sorry. Do you mean that I should change...'

> 9. *A:* Give me that calculator.
>
> *B:* Who was your servant last year?
>
> *A:* Sorry. I don't understand.
>
> *B:* Never mind. (*laughs*)
>
> *A:* (*laughs*)

Analysis: Both the *language* and *communicative styles* are presenting a problem. B appears to have interpreted A's utterance as an inappropriate request. He tries to indicate the inappropriateness by a fairly light-hearted indirect strategy. Because it is very indirect and highly culture-specific, he unfortunately compounds the problem. The source of the initial problem here could either be linguistic (A wants to make a request, but has not used linguistic tools that B would recognise as acceptable, such as 'please' or 'could you...', etc.) or it could be cultural (A assumes that it is not necessary to use a politeness strategy in asking a colleague for a minor piece of assistance).

Repair: B could use more direct strategies. A could persist a little to investigate the meaning of and reason behind the 'servant' comment, or could ask a third party after the event.

10. *A:* Well, I think that just about wraps it up.

  B: Sorry?

Analysis: Language is creating a problem, stemming from the idiom 'to wrap something up' (= 'to finish or complete').

Repair: A needs to rephrase her statement, with a less idiomatic expression. In future, she might avoid such idioms or perhaps use idioms with explanations. B needs to do some linguistic research, either by immediately seeking clarification: 'Sorry. What was that word you used just now?' or by asking a third party subsequently.

11. (*Extract from school letter to parents*) As part of our special activities next week we will be asking all mothers to come and meet their child's teacher in the main hall. This will give them an opportunity to discuss their child's progress.

Analysis: The problem lies in *different assumptions.* This school policy decision has potential for conflict in cultural values/assumptions. Some of the parents may feel it is inappropriate for the mothers to do this (it should be the fathers, for example, or both parents together, or perhaps an older sibling, whose command of the language is better).

Repair: Unless the school specifically wants the mothers only (in which case, they might need to be ready to do some explaining and negotiating), they should build more flexibility into their plan (e.g. 'a family member or representative').

12. (*In class*)

  A: Have you finished your assignment?

  B: No, sir.

  A: You haven't done your assignment?!

  B: Yes, sir.

  A: (*Looks puzzled*)

Analysis: The problem here is clearly *linguistic.* In A's language, presumably you confirm the accuracy of a negative question by saying 'no', whereas in B's language such confirmation is done with a 'yes' (which, incidentally, is the more common pattern world-wide).

Repair: Both A and B (but perhaps especially B, given that she is the student in this situation) need to do some linguistic research.

13. (TV commercial) A stylishly dressed young woman faces the camera and says, smilingly: He let me choose the apartment. He let me buy our new car. He even lets me buy his clothes. Her expression then becomes more irritated as she continues: But he won't let me join his friends for a Gold Star Cognac. In the background we now see a group of men drinking cognac. The woman continues speaking as she walks to her car: So I've decided to leave him... Her expression changes to a smile as she says... just for tonight, and drives away.

Analysis: Different cultural values and assumptions are at work here. This is a slight adaptation of an actual commercial. In some cultures this would be regarded as unacceptably sexist (that is, it unjustly assigns roles and behaviour according to gender). Sexism is, of course, a highly culture-specific concept.

Repair: The company would probably have to change the commercial if it were to consider running it in other markets. Conversely, tribes who find it offensive could remind themselves that there are other ways of looking at gender roles, even if they don't like them.

14. When I was a newcomer to this company, my boss treated me in a very friendly way. This was my first job in a Belgian company, and I was impressed that he tried to show concern for his subordinates. I thought he was a really good person and not picky. I didn't give my opinion, but just obeyed his instructions and did whatever I could. After one year, I had my first review and it was an absolute shock for me. His evaluation of me was pretty negative and that was totally different from what I expected. How could he treat me so nicely and yet write a review that was quite negative? I don't know what to do.

Analysis: The source of the problem is values and communicative styles. The worker seems to have made a few unjustified assumptions, including that friendliness excludes the possibility of a negative evaluation and that the absence of critical comment means satisfaction with his performance — all of which, of course, may be true in his own culture.

Repair: He could try a few more explicit strategies, to check what is required of him, how he will be evaluated, and what progress he is making.

15. Read the following cartoon. If you feel that you understand it completely, decide what aspects of culture and language could cause problems for a reader from a different culture. If you don't understand this cartoon, try to pinpoint what is causing the problem.

Analysis: Language could cause problems, e.g. 'yeah' = 'yes'; 'blaze away' = 'go ahead'; 'cripes' = an expression of slight dismay, something like 'oh, dear' because he is contemplating a difficult and complex answer; 'footy' = 'football'; 'the trots'

= a form of horse racing; 'em' = 'them'; 'offhand' = 'without prior preparation'; 'sorta' = 'sort of'; 'the box' = 'television'; 'darl' = 'darling' (presumably his wife). Cultural knowledge presents potential difficulty; 'survey' — in this society it is common for government institutions and private companies to conduct telephone surveys to determine people's views and preferences; 'son' — he is referring in an informal and friendly way to the younger man (not, of course, his son) who is conducting the survey. Values may present problems: There is a cultural value which the man should understand, but doesn't: namely that it is more desirable to actually play sport than merely watch it on television. The man misunderstands the intended meaning of 'involved' (= 'play/actively participate in'), assuming that it means 'be interested'. A character's failure to understand what the reader automatically understands is often a source of humour (perhaps in many cultures). The joke is that, although the man claims to be very 'involved' in sport, he is actually so unfit and lazy that he asks his wife to hang up the telephone for him. If this explanation is not clear to you, it merely demonstrates what you probably know already, namely that humour can be very culture-specific (and difficult to 'translate')!

Repair: None is necessary, but of course the authors would need to understand that its audience may be restricted.

- When something is going awry in communication, don't blame the people involved. Look for the problem.
- Problems in intercultural communication usually involve language hitches, differences in communication style, or differences in values and expectations.

Let's move on to more serious matters. Perhaps one of the more important issues capable of analysis is prejudice, a widespread phenomenon even in those cultures which value its elimination. It deserves some scrutiny .

'Prejudice' is making judgments about individuals based purely on their group memberships (for example, their gender, ethnicity, occupation, education, religion, and so on). Strictly speaking, 'prejudice' can involve either positive or negative assumptions, although its negative connotation is more common.

Prejudice should be distinguished from 'discrimination', which is the imposition of some kind of unfair, unequal treatment because of prejudicial views. The distinction is critical. In the following task, ask yourself whether the individuals are victims of prejudice (an unpleasant but very common phenomenon, resulting from the universal tendency towards group memberships) or victims of discrimination (an unacceptable phenomenon, at least to many people in many tribes)?

Read the following article, 'Managing at work', written in 1987 by a newspaper columnist, Andrew Grove at the San Jose Mercury, who is responding to questions from two readers.

Q: What should I do if I find prejudice against me at work? I am a foreigner. My new supervisor doesn't like foreign people. She gives me harder jobs to do without clear explanation. I think she does it so she can get rid of me more easily when I cannot do the job well.

Q: I am a foreigner. I got a production job. My attendance has been perfect. When the company needs some work finished, I always volunteer to do it after 5 p.m. My boss is very happy when I do that and he is very nice to me. But my co-workers dislike me (except some who sit next to me). I try to be nice to them but they don't treat me like a friend. I cannot find out why and don't know what to do about it.

A: No country provides as much opportunity to the foreign-born as the United States. Still, even here, being an immigrant carries its special difficulties.

Prejudice against foreigners is one of those difficulties, but I believe other problems are often mistaken for it. Perhaps the first reader's supervisor isn't prejudiced at all, just tired of fighting a language barrier. To a foreign employee, the two may appear to be the same. Perhaps the second reader's co-workers don't really dislike him. Maybe they don't have as much in common with him as with other fellow employees and are not inclined — or don't know how — to make the extra effort to include him in their conversations...

But whether it is prejudice or something else matters little to these two individuals who are trying to make their way in a new world. The fact is that in addition to the difficulties any employee or job applicant faces, these readers have at least one in addition because of being foreign.

People with an extra load to carry merit a little help from those around them. I know from my own experience that there are many Americans ready to go the extra step and lend a hand to people like them. Please do!

Our two readers, however, cannot count on this to happen. They must go on with their lives as best they can. What they need is more patience and extra perseverance.

To the first reader: don't assume people are prejudiced toward you. On the contrary, assume they are not; ignore it if you must — there is nothing, really, that you can do about it.

To the second reader: be patient. You cannot force friendships. They either come on their own or not at all. Go on with your work, be friendly and open, and respond to friendly gestures if they come, but don't chase after your fellow workers.

Do you agree with the columnist's advice? What do you think of the following comments from his column? If you disagree, what is your view? If you would like to compare your own views with someone else's, I've put my reactions under each comment. Of course, they are personal opinions only.

1. 'being an immigrant carries its special difficulties'

   Agree. Immigrants certainly do have specific challenges in the workplace that native-born workers do not have. These include (in some cases) the necessity of operating in a second language, the necessity of becoming familiar with a different 'work culture', and (in some cases) the existence of prejudice. Naturally, even native-born workers will in some cases be quite familiar with the second and third of these problems!

2. 'don't assume people are prejudiced toward you'; 'other problems are often mistaken for (prejudice)'

   Agree. Check it out first. An assumption that your co-workers are prejudiced is of course itself a form of prejudice. (Also, it is surely important for any of us to try to be free of prejudice ourselves before we start complaining about prejudice against us.)

3. 'Perhaps the first reader's supervisor isn't prejudiced at all, just tired of fighting a language barrier.'

   Agree. This is a possible explanation. If I were in this situation, I would check it out: 'Excuse me, could I talk to you for a minute about my job here?… Do you find that language is a problem when we communicate?… Are there any other aspects of my job performance that you could give me some feedback on?… etc.'

4. 'there is nothing, really, that you can do about it.'

   Disagree. If this American reader became convinced that he was the victim of discrimination, as distinct from prejudice (as defined on page

113) he most certainly could (i) confront the person in question, or (ii) (depending on the nature and impact of that discrimination) consider making a formal complaint within his company or ultimately even take legal action, if this alternative is available. You can't stop people being prejudiced against you, but you can try to stop them discriminating ('She gives me harder jobs to do.').

5. 'Go on with your work, be friendly and open, and respond to friendly gestures if they come, but don't chase after your fellow workers.'

    Partially agree. Certainly, in any culture one doesn't usually 'chase after' co-workers' friendship. There is, however, something, more proactive that he can do (apart from the sensible advice of being friendly — although 'being friendly' of course varies from culture to culture.) You can take on a (long-term, if necessary) research task in intercultural awareness: What do these people talk about? Who tends to group with whom? Why? How do these people initiate casual conversation? etc, etc.

6. What they need is more patience and extra perseverance.

    Partially agree. See 1, above, but also see 5.

Prejudice and discrimination are difficult phenomena. Government legislation and workplace regulations can reduce the latter; the former involves individual efforts — and is much harder to reduce.

- ✖ Prejudice will disappear if we just 'wish it away'.
- ✔ Reducing prejudice requires the expansion of individual experience, skill, and attitude.

I referred above to the need to identify the critical characteristics of a culture (rather than trying to 'understand' everything about a culture):

'The major task facing a sojourner is not to adjust to a new culture, but to learn its salient characteristics.'[3]

What might these characteristics be? It is impossible to provide a general answer. Not only will the answer depend on intercultural goals, but it will also inevitably reflect individual and ethnocentric bias. Here, for what it is worth, are the characteristics that I have found to be relatively critical in my intercultural situations. Remember: they are both personal and ethnocentric:

- solidarity and deference strategies for getting people to do things
- openings and closings
- relative value given to individualism versus collectivism
- the role of power-distance in interactions.

Only through monitoring and analysis of your intercultural situation(s) will you be able to determine the critical characteristics which require your focused attention.

MONITORING SKILLS: KEEPING AN EYE ON HOW THINGS ARE GOING

A prerequisite for developing monitoring skills is that we have externalisation skills and analytical skills.

In the section above, we have stressed the role of analysis in successful intercultural communication. This should not, however, be taken to imply that we need to monitor every utterance we produce or receive, every gesture we emit or see, every value we encode or decode. That is impossible, unrealistic, unnecessary — and probably very irritating and exhausting! In short, don't over-analyse and don't over-monitor.

Communication, even within one culture, is a lot messier than we tend to think it is. Perhaps influenced by reading plays and novels and seeing dialogue on film, we may believe that communication is clean and linear, whereas transcripts of actual communication show a far more disjointed structure full of slips, overlaps and fragments. Communication is less deliberate and less conscious than many of us tend to think. Although guided by bed-rock 'norms', we appear to proceed through our interactions rather 'holistically', not in deliberate step-by-step fashion.[4]

If this assumption is true, then our monitoring of communication should generally not be at the level of the word or the sentence, but rather at a 'higher' level, where we are asking ourselves questions like:

- What, overall, am I trying to achieve here?
- What's he getting at?
- How am I feeling about this communication?
- How does he seem to be feeling about this communication?
- Do we seem to be succeeding?

To use a computer analogy, we need to subject communication to an occasional 'page-view' — where we can see the overall shape of the text, but not the individual words. If we were to subject every word as it is added to a pageview, we would never produce any texts. Try it yourself on a computer and see how long you can sustain it!

If you are not familiar with the computer analogy, try this. Monitoring intercultural communication involves 'leaning back in your chair' to see what is going on, rather than always leaning forward to scrutinise the details.

Yet another analogy: If you have any experience with doing jigsaw puzzles, you will know that there needs to be a combination of leaning forward and leaning back if you are to make progress.

One writer has talked of the 'observer stance', where her aim is 'simply to be more aware of what is going on and not biased by my own cultural predispositions and expectations'.[5]

✐ Stand 'outside' your communication and try to see how it's going.

Watch a television program (a film, say, or a comedy series or a documentary) with the volume turned off. See how much you can understand from the body language and the context — and of course your considerable knowledge of the behavioural norms of your culture. If possible, then watch a television programme from a different language/culture, and do the same.

Similarly, we should not seek to 'repair' every problem we spot. That is neither feasible nor necessary; communication would collapse with over-repair.

How often, then, should one monitor and repair? Naturally, that will depend on what is at stake, one of the issues we look at in the next section.

COMMUNICATION SKILLS: AVOIDING PROBLEMS AND REPAIRING PROBLEMS

A prerequisite for developing communication skills is that we have externalisation skills, analytical skills, and monitoring skills.

Ultimately, our main aim has to be to avoid miscommunication (if possible) and repair miscommunication (if possible and if necessary).

An approach which avoids, or at least minimises, the possibility of miscommunication will clearly be useful in intercultural communication. I will call this approach 'prepair' (assuming that your value system allows me to tamper with English and create a new word). It contrasts with 'repair', where we fix a problem that has already happened.

To illustrate prepair and repair strategies, let's return to the 'divorce example':

Eks: And your wife, Mr Wai?

Wai: Actually, I'm divorced.

Eks: Oh, what a pity. What happened?

Wai: Well...

In his second utterance ('Oh, what a pity. What happened?') Eks has gone for an ALPHA behaviour. He assumes that this topic and his approach to the topic are universally accepted. One prepair strategy, sensing that the topic might not be universally open to exploration, would be to avoid comment entirely, or provide a minimal comment, such as 'Oh, I see', and move to change the topic.

Are there alternative prepair strategies available to him, where he can maintain the topic (thus keeping his culture-specific interest), but minimise the risk of mutual loss of face? Given what you know of solidarity and deference politeness strategies, how might he minimise any difficulties? ('I hope you don't mind me asking, but...') Turning to Mr Wai, we have already noted (page 102) that he can externalise and can speculate about alternative ways of seeing the issue. But how does he repair the situation — and should he repair?

Possible repair strategies include the following:

- Depersonalise and go off-record, by saying something like 'Yes. Well, that's life isn't it?'

- Go entirely off-record and break the link between one utterance and the next, by saying something like 'Yes, we were divorced about ten years ago.'
- Go on-record about the topic choice (but totally avoiding the required 'content' response), by saying something like: 'I'm very sorry. People from my country find it very difficult to talk about these things.' (Note the deference politeness). 'Tell me, is divorce very common here in your country?' In this way the link is maintained.
- Go on-record (baldly) and say something like 'That's none of your business.'

Note that, in all of these alternatives, Mr Wai has not had to abandon his own culture. In the first and second alternatives, he has retained his cultural priority, namely to retain private control over such matters as divorce. Similarly, his adjustment in the third alternative has not 'betrayed' his value system — and might even lead to an interesting and enjoyable exchange about culture. In the last (and most ethnocentric) alternative, he has however, potentially caused bewilderment and conflict.

Should there be a shift, either in prepair or repair? Of course it depends; there is really no general answer. It will depend on the parties involved, the circumstances, the stakes. What is the cost/effort/risk involved compared with the potential benefits of the strategy? Only the two particular parties in a communication can answer the question.

Who should perform the shift? Similarly, there can be no standard answer. It will depend on the relative power structure of the parties, the circumstances of the communication, and — inevitably — the relative skill of the communicators.

In reviewing just two of the situations described above, for example:

(i) Should the person upset by being told he has gained weight communicate his feelings or accept the situation?

(ii) In the job interview example, should the interviewer or the interviewee make an adjustment to the other's expectations?

Most important to note is that within our own cultures we all perform both prepair and repair. We have seen many examples of this in people communicating off-record and in using solidarity and deference strategies, reducing the risk of failure in achieving their communication goal. Similarly, people are familiar with repair strategies, spotting problems and moving to keep the communication on track.

In everyday interactions within our own culture, we constantly adjust our communication according to how we perceive the requirements of the situation and the person with whom we are communicating. Factors such as his knowledge of the subject, his interest in the topic, and his emotional reaction will influence how we 'build' our communication. Consider the following simple example, where A and B (a customer and a sales clerk, respectively) are both native speakers of the same language:

A: I'd like to buy a computer.

B: Sure. What did you have in mind? A laptop?

A: Pardon?

B: Have you had a computer before?

Here B has made a repair once he realises that A does not recognise the word 'laptop' as a type of computer.

The rest of this section is devoted to looking at prepair and repair strategies.

The first dimension that might need prepair/repair in communication is a purely linguistic one. For example, I might avoid using the word '*kinesics*' when talking to my family. If I do use it — and I see that there is a comprehension problem — I would repair it, by rephrasing it as 'body language'.

A partner in cross-cultural communication may need to keep making language adjustments in the exchange. Cross-cultural communication often — though not always — means that one of the communication partners is operating outside their native language. Sometimes *neither* partner is using a native language: to take just one example, a Japanese businessman talking with a Venezuelan client in English.

The main prepair strategies (for a linguistic problem) are *selection* and *positioning*.

The first of these is to select words that are more likely to be understood and avoid words that might cause difficulty. Apart from technical words and jargon, these may include slang and idioms. You are probably quite sensitive to what constitutes slang in your language (highly informal, 'non-standard' words and expressions), but you may be less sensitive to idioms.

Idioms occur when words are put together to form a different combined meaning: that is:

a + b = c (*NOT* ab)

For example: 'to give up' in English means something quite different from the sum of the two words, 'give' and 'up'.

How might you avoid the following English idioms and slang in communication (if you felt it was necessary to do so)?

● What time do you *knock off*?

● They *knocked back* our proposal.

● I think we should *give it a go*.

● He really *lost his temper*.

It is not necessarily the case, however, that a non-native speaker will be more familiar with the standard language code than the idiomatic. It will depend very much on the individual speaker's background. Don't pre-judge.

- When I was working in a restaurant in Zurich, Swiss customers assumed, judging from my appearance, that I was Swiss and would address me in Swiss German. I had learnt German at school in Australia and could not understand their dialect (which is quite different), so inevitably would have to ask them to repeat everything in standard German. By contrast, the Swiss customers usually addressed the Egyptian and Turkish waiters in standard German, whereas they could speak only Swiss German! Again, everything had to be repeated.

Of course we do more than select and reject words when we speak. We also can select a particular volume of speech, a degree of clarity in our articulation, a range of body language, a certain quantity and quality of speaking. All of these can be 'pre-paired' to maximise the chances for successful communication.

The second strategy in effective prepair is positioning. One type of positioning is to bring the topic of our utterances to the front. For example: Instead of 'Excuse me. I'm afraid we're a bit lost. Could you tell me where the X market is? ', position your topic at the beginning and say 'Excuse me. The X Market. Where is it, please?' (without damaging the language or your concept of appropriate politeness).

Let's assume that the following piece of communication caused difficulty. How could it have been rephrased to avoid, or at least minimise, the difficulty?

- Well, we've given your proposal every possible consideration — I think I can say that in all fairness — and we've come up with a number of, well... concerns that we'd like to bring to your attention.

Note: Wrecking the language and shouting are not appropriate strategies. They are two instances of what linguists call 'foreigner talk'.

Where a language problem does occur and needs repair, the two most common strategies are rephrasing (see example 1) and paraphrasing (see example 2). Examples 3 and 4 present unacceptable repair strategies.

1. A: To be frank, they thought the unit cost was far too dear.
    B: Sorry?
    A: They thought the unit price was too expensive.
    B: Oh, I see.

2. A: To be frank, they thought the unit cost was far too dear.
    B: Sorry?
    A: They thought the unit cost — you know, the price per item — was too expensive.
    B: Oh, I see.

3. *A:* To be frank, they thought the unit cost was far too dear.
   B: Sorry?
   A: They think unit cost too dear.
   B: Oh, ...

4. *A:* To be frank, they thought it was far too dear.
   B: Sorry?
   A: They thought the unit cost was (*louder*) far too dear.
   B: Yes?

How would you rank the following workplace signs according to how likely they would be to succeed communicatively in a multicultural workplace. Why have you ranked them in this order?

1. (*On a building site*)
   (a) Safety helmets must be worn at all times.
   (b) Always wear your safety helmet.
   (c) Safety helmets save lives.

2. (*In an office, near the photocopier*)
   (a) Copying whole books is a breach of copyright law!
   (b) It is against the law to copy all of a book!
   (c) Before you photocopy that book, think about the copyright law!

A final word about language in intercultural communication, especially when it involves a native speaker and a non-native speaker. There is a widespread tendency, which is probably found in all cultures, to make judgements about a person's intelligence or sophistication based on their performance in a non-native language. It is essential for all of us to 'look through' the imperfect language to see the person.

Perhaps this is particularly important for monolingual speakers of English as a native language, since they generally have to make fewer shifts, internationally, than speakers of other languages. They may, therefore, not have much experience with the frustrating constraints on self-expression that can occur when operating outside their first language.

Throughout Chapter 2, we saw that communication consists of far more than words (however they are selected and positioned).

All cultures make adjustments to acknowledge the power or status of a communication partner. Consider how students talk to their teachers (compared with how they talk to one another), or how staff address the boss (as opposed to a colleague), or how you might talk to your prospective father-in-law (as opposed to a prospective younger sister-in-law).

Similarly, we can also adjust our communication to fit the cultural expectations and knowledge of the other person, as the following task illustrates. Consider the following exchange:

A: Pleased to meet you.

B: Siregar.

A: Sorry?

B: My name is Siregar. How do you do.

A: Yes. How do you do.

What do people in Siregar's culture do when they meet somebody for the first time? Clearly, they give their name only. Which person knows aspects of both cultures and who has made an adjustment: A or B? (Clearly, it is B.)

In general, who should make the adjustment?

- Should Mr Siregar (in the example above) persist with his culture-specific method of self-introduction and repeat his name only, or, realising A is 'lost', make an adjustment?

- Should the Japanese businessman shake hands with the American businessman or should the American bow when he meets the former? (Power is relevant. It is interesting to note the number of business people from English-speaking countries who know, and sometimes use, the Japanese honorific, while very few know the equivalent for a Thai or Indonesian businessman.)

There are of course no easy 'answers' to these questions. The critical factors in the decision are similar to the factors we would recognise in the sales clerk's situation above — or the prospective son-in-law or the staff member talking to her boss. The relationship between the two people and relative power of the two people are clearly critical factors. Of course, in an intercultural situation the factors will be more complex and may require quite demanding adjustments in both attitude and language.

The kind of linguistic prepair/repair we've seen above can be applied more broadly, aiming to make our *communication* — not just our language — clearer, more appropriate, and more acceptable.

Here the primary strategy, both in prepair and repair, is *being explicit.*

Before we look at this strategy, it should be noted that being explicit does not mean being terse or blunt! Like any other communicative act, 'being explicit' can be performed with softening action. It can be 'modulated, softened and adapted to particular circumstances of role, deference, size of imposition, protection of solidarity and saving of face'.[6] Both solidarity and deference strategies are available. As we saw in the 'fronting' strategy above, the essentials are retained, and comprehensibility is enhanced.

In terms of *pre*pair, being explicit means making your intention, your purpose, your viewpoint as clear as possible to your communication partner. One researcher calls this a 'playing-it-safe strategy of communication'. What you are doing is *establishing*, rather than *presupposing* common ground (as we so often can do within our own culture).

Which of the following two alternatives more explicitly establishes the speaker's intention?

- Your report needs a few changes, I'm afraid. Can we go through them together now? OK? Three things, probably. Now, let's see. First, the title page. Could you please add some...

- I was going through your report and there were some things that I had a bit of difficulty with, to be honest. The title page, for example. I noticed that there wasn't any...

The first approach is more explicit. The speaker's intention (that the listener make some changes) is clearer. Notice that he has used several deference politeness strategies; again, explicit doesn't necessarily mean blunt.

Which of these two alternatives more explicitly establishes the topic and 'bridges' to a previous relevant utterance?

- I'd just like to add my support to what Mr Eks said about the delivery schedule. I also feel that November is...

- I just wanted to say that I also feel that November is unrealistic given the production targets.

Which of the following pair more explicitly establishes the purpose of the communication? Clearly, the second alternative.

- (*On the telephone*) Yes. Good morning. I bought a clock radio in your store yesterday — you had them on sale — and, well, I can't get it to work. I've looked at the instructions carefully, but. Anyway, I'm really not very happy about it.

- (*On the telephone*) Yes. Good morning. I'd like to speak to someone about getting a refund, please. I bought a clock radio from your store yesterday and it isn't working properly.

Devise a more explicit version of the following pieces of communication. As you do so, decide how much softening action (if any) you want to take in the communication.

- 'If you persist with this kind of behaviour, there could be consequences.'
- 'I'm not saying that the whole report has to be re-written, but I can't see you avoiding some major revisions.'

One useful explicitising strategy is *labelling communication*. Here the speaker overtly describes her purpose, intention or expectation to her listener. Here are some examples:[7]

- My question is this...
- Can I ask you something?
- I just want to check...
- Let me tell you exactly what I want...
- Can I ask you a favour?
- Could I give an opinion on that?
- This is how I would explain it...

Without these explicit signals, the listener has to decide the speaker's intention from the information provided. Interculturally (especially where one or both people are operating outside their first language), this may cause problems.

Often our listener (or reader) doesn't know where we are heading. For example, what interpretations could be formed in the following communication,[8] at the points marked (a), (b) and (c)? When you reach each of these points, stop and ask yourself what the purpose of the communication is, and where it's heading:

My husband and I are Indian nationals who have been resident in Hong Kong for several years. (a)

We take annual leave each summer and this year decided that it would be nice to spend a couple of days in the Maldives and Sri Lanka to break our journey back to Hong Kong. (b)

Airline schedules being what they are, we soon discovered that although we only wanted to stop over for two days in Sri Lanka on the return leg of our trip, it was necessary to spend 10 hours in Colombo, albeit in transit, on our outward journey. (c)

Where is the communication heading? A further ten (very articulate) paragraphs reveal that it is a complaint about the service of a particular Consulate in issuing visas.

Of course, when operating within our language within our own tribe, we can usually cope very well with an absence of overt communication signals. In this particular case, the reader is helped by seeing that the communication occurs on the 'letters to the editor' page of a newspaper — which triggers certain expectations of the content and intent of the communication — and by the heading ('Arrogant and unhelpful') provided by the editor.

The expectations we have for how an event, including a communicative event, will tend to unfold is quite culture-specific. These programmed expectations — one of the technical terms for them is 'scripts' — help us manage our behaviour and communication more easily. In the case of social events, this point is quite easy to see. You could write the script for a business meeting in your tribe, but could you write a script for, say, an Indonesian business meeting? Perhaps it is a little more difficult to see for communicative acts (such as a letter to an editor, or a university lecture, or a consultation with a doctor), but these are just as culture-bound as the business meeting example.

If you don't have a script for a particular event in another culture, or if your script differs from that culture's script, then intercultural difficulties can occur.

- At some universities in Australia, lecturers are being encouraged to make their lecture 'scripts' more explicit, because of the number of foreign students in their classes. Explicit strategies in this case include such routines as: 'First, I will look at...'; 'These are the main points...'; 'Now I will analyse...'.

Explicitness can refer not only to the content of the communication itself. A speaker can step outside the content and explicitly *declare difficulty*. The difficulty might be in:

- understanding the content ('Sorry, I don't understand.')
- understanding the intention ('I'm sorry. I can't quite see what you're getting at.')
- accepting the appropriateness of the communication ('Sorry. People in my culture find it very difficult to talk about divorce.')

Naturally, the examples given here could be presented with more or less softening action.

These three strategies are just a few possible expressions of a general *clarifying* strategy — in which we attempt to make something explicitly clear.

Other possibilities include clarifying:

1. a speaker's intention
2. the topic under discussion
3. the relevance of an utterance to previous utterances
4. a speaker's underlying assumptions or values
5. the stage which an exchange has reached
6. a speaker's expectations (for the listener)

What are the following clarifying strategies seeking to clarify? Refer to the list 1–6, just above. I have given my analysis after each example.

(a) Yes, I do understand what you're saying... But I don't quite see how you'd like me to help on this. (6. *Clarifying a speaker's expectations for the listener.*)

(b) I follow what you mean ... Except, how does Marlene's holiday pay come into it? (3. *Clarifying the relevance of an utterance to previous utterances.*)

(c) OK, I get the general picture, but what isn't clear to me is why is that a problem? (4. *Clarifying a speaker's underlying assumptions or values.*)

(d) Are we taking about Volume 1 or Volume II? (2. *Clarifying the topic under discussion.*)

(e) Well, I think we've heard all the arguments on both sides of the issue. Are there any more comments before we move to a decision? (5. *Clarifying the stage which an exchange has reached.*)

(f) Sorry. You want my opinion? (6. *Clarifying a speaker's expectations for the listener.*)

(g) Let me get this straight. We'll go that way only if they reject our offer? (1. *Clarifying a speaker's intention.*)

Again, please note that these are examples only.[9] In *your* communication situations, you may feel that you need to take more (or perhaps less) softening action in performing your clarifications.

If, when operating interculturally, you are not using your first language, it is particularly important to master the range of language routines and communication strategies you can use in *clarifying*. The actual routines will, of course, vary from language to language, but the strategies are probably universal. Here are some of the possibilities, exemplified in English:

- Declare partial or total non-comprehension, which is usually an 'off-record' strategy for seeking clarification — 'Sorry. I don't understand'.

- Indicate the part of the communication which you need clarified — 'What is a "phoneme"?' 'Sorry, when you say "as soon as possible"...'

- Use an 'on-record' strategy seeking clarification, either baldly ('What?') or with softening action ('Could you possibly explain what you mean?').

- Confirm your understanding by repeating relevant parts of the prior communication — 'Pick up at nine o'clock — right?'.

- Confirm your understanding by reformulating the prior communication in your own words — 'So, if we don't get this contract, we're really in trouble. Is that what you're saying?'.

Most languages probably have a word equivalent to the English '*what?*' In your tribe are there any constraints on its use as a clarifying strategy? (Many English speakers, for example, have been socialised to limit its use.)

Clarifying strategies do more than potentially raise the level of comprehension. By intervening in the communication to clarify, the speaker can gain a measure of power, presenting herself as *co-manager* of the exchange. This may be particularly important if the speaker is operating in her second language, where her linguistic resources cannot match the native speaker's.

For example: Consider the supervisor on page 105 who, in orienting a new staff member, told him to come and see him any time if he had problems. The worker in this instance could — if he felt it important enough — seek to clarify the supervisor's statement ('I'm sorry. Do you mean that I will have problems?') or seek subsequent advice from someone more familiar than he is with the supervisor's culture.

Clarification is not, of course, confined to responses to the other speaker's questions. We can clarify proactively, before we proceed in our communication. Here are some examples:

- Sorry. What should I call you?
- How would you prefer to do this?
- If I could ask… What exactly are you looking for in the essay due next month?

Similarly, we can seek to clarify our own meaning, making it more comprehensible and explicit for our listener (or reader), and repairing our own communication. We do this by defining and rephrasing our content as we proceed. Here are some examples:

- In other words, I'd like you to…
- He bought a palmtop — you know, one of those new computers that fit into the palm of your hand.
- It's divided into four parts — no, that doesn't sound right — what I mean is…

Now look back at some of the repairs and prepairs we've seen in this chapter (e.g. on pp.102–110). Are there any that you would find completely unacceptable? Which of them would you regard as real 'changes', that is, fundamental shifts in your value system and principles?

This is not to trivialise the difficulty in intercultural communication. Indeed, there are times when we are compelled by circumstances to make quite profound modifications. It is surely important, at the same time, to recognise that many of them are adjustments, rather than changes, leaving our cultures intact — which is what the vast majority of us want.

Not that you can (or would want to) apply clarifying strategies in *all* situations. Consider the following:

A: Good morning. Can I help you?

B: I want to see Mr Eks.

A: Yes. (*looks irritated*) Do you have an appointment?

B's opening strategy does not seem to meet A's expectations. Although successful in its explicitness, perhaps it is too 'bald' and needs redressive softening. If B is operating in his first language, perhaps the source of the problem is purely linguistic, selecting 'want' rather then the conventionally softer 'would like'. Presumably his facial gestures and other body language did not redress the baldness of the communication. As with all second-language learners, B would do well to pay particular attention to learning routine openings, especially when these involve requests. Of course, it is possible that B's value system and perception of power-distance are also relevant here. This may be relevant to decisions about repair strategies. In any case, an immediate repair strategy here seems unnecessary, although B would do well to note the reaction to his communication (if possible), and do some subsequent investigation.

There seems little that A can do, either in terms of prepair and repair. Emotionally, he could, however, try to minimise any negative reactions he feels, if B is clearly from another culture and is not using his native language. He should be aware that B may well be intending to achieve the *goal* that A himself shares (i.e. polite, successful communication). The problem is with *means* only.

Try one more example:

A: Where did you get the new computer?
B: Oh, I got it at Reid's the other day. My friend George helped me pick it out.
A: George? I don't think I know him. Where does he work?
B: I don't know.
A: I thought you said he was your friend.
B: Yes, he is.
A: Oh. Yeah, well… it's a nice computer.

Clearly the two cultures differ in their interpretation of what constitutes a 'friend'. It probably doesn't require any repair, but both A and B could — if this were appropriate in their relationship — declare their confusion and explore their different concepts of 'friendship'.

So, *where possible and where appropriate,* try to…

- externalise (don't assume); minimise ethnocentricity
- monitor the *gist* of what speakers are saying
- monitor how the speakers are feeling
- analyse the speakers' perceptions, values, communication styles and strategies
- minimise language problems by selecting and structuring your content to match the other person's competence in the language
- explicitly state your meaning, your purpose, your intention, your topic, the relevance of your communication to previous utterances, your expectations for the listener, your assumptions, your value priorities
- 'label' what you are doing in your communication
- provide relevant background information
- declare difficulty with the other person's communication (his speed, his intention, his topic choice)

- *✍* clarify the speaker's meaning, purpose, intention, topic, value priorities, expectations, and relevance to previous communication
- *✍* repair misunderstandings by making explicit statements
- *✍* provide signals to your listener(s) to show what stage you are up to in your communication.

ANXIETY MANAGEMENT SKILLS: RESOLVING THE EMOTIONAL ASPECTS

A prerequisite for developing anxiety management skills is that we have externalisation skills, analytical skills, monitoring skills, and communication skills.

Interpersonal communications, even within one tribe, can be accompanied by anxiety. When communicators are also dealing with the complexities of cultural differences, this anxiety can be even greater, especially when it involves a long-term sojourn into another culture.

It has been suggested that the *severity* of stress levels depends on a range of factors, including previous experience, 'cultural distance' (how different is the new culture), and individual personality differences.[10]

On first contact, this anxiety is called 'culture shock', which can be defined as 'the confusion resulting from well-established habits no longer having their expected consequences'.[11] Research has shown that culture shock can lead to quite serious physical and psychological illness and can be quite prolonged. Except, perhaps, for tourists and short-term visitors (neither of whom have to really 'engage' the local culture in any depth), all people can expect to experience culture shock, although some people do deny that they are experiencing it.

If you have never experienced culture shock, may I offer the following sample. The extracts are taken from my journal in the first period after moving to a foreign country. It should be noted that (unlike many immigrants) I had a job to come to, and that (again, unlike many immigrants) I belonged to a fairly powerful minority in this country. What I had in common with many immigrants, however, was that my emigration was associated with a painful personal separation.

After one week:

> You can't process all the information you're confronted with. My 'processor' can't take in all the data at once... Kaplan had it all wrong with his J-curve of the settlement experience (euphoria, then depression, then adjustment, and finally, acceptance). There certainly isn't necessarily an initial honeymoon phase. I suspect that that view is influenced by ethnocentric assumptions — 'of course they're euphoric to be here'. What would I call this initial phase? Probably 'disorientation'... Dealing with your own group (in my

case, the Western expatriates) is the first task of the settler… I feel a need to be listened to. I don't want to talk about the future. (Cheerful encouragement from people about exciting local events in the coming months leaves me numb.) My time frame is today. I want to talk about how I got this far. Why I came, how I felt when I arrived, how I feel now, how I managed to find the right train to get here today. I want my achievements noted (yes, even getting the right train). I don't feel my usual respect for balance in communication. I'm putting all my energy into myself… Empathy strategies don't work for me. 'Yes, I remember when I first arrived, I …' I want people to talk less, question less, listen more, let me control topics more… The opening questions are particularly irritating. 'How long have you been here?' sounds like a value judgement; 'Where are you from?' becomes tedious and feels irrelevant (I feel like I'm being processed); the expatriate question 'Where have you been?' is certainly a value judgement. I'd prefer: 'How's it going?'; 'What are you finding difficult?'; 'Are there things you want me to tell you about?' Understand that you can't understand what I'm going through.

After four weeks:

I can see things now, and notice details… All senses — having been suspended, disrupted, reshuffled — have now settled. I can now see everything (and I see it differently). Visual norms have shifted: what is attractive, crowded, clear, acceptable, desirable — all of these are now altered and settled. I can process information more efficiently now. I can listen and hear. I can talk to people, and topics don't matter. I can share… Like clay on a potter's wheel, some of the stuff (feelings/experiences/sensations) has spun off and been discarded. There's now a workable pot come out it. But some of the clay still doesn't fit in the shape of the pot and I can't discard it. It sits there, growing smaller and harder — unresolved.

After seven weeks:

The agenda is different now after this number of weeks. In some ways, it's smaller, less overwhelming. In other ways, it's larger. I'm turning now, from settlement to living… I'm sure I won't even remember what the settlement phase was like. Odd flashes perhaps.

Have you experienced anything similar? Which of the journal observations do you think you could take into account if you were my colleague or my boss?

What can one do about culture shock or indeed the day-to-day anxiety associated with any kind of intercultural situation?

The first answer is one of awareness. Understand that it is a natural process that does not reflect on your intelligence or strength and which should not be allowed to influence your self-esteem.

In more strategic terms, the following are necessary:

- externalise, and recognise the existence of intercultural anxiety
- monitor its development
- analyse its sources
- (where possible) communicate your anxiety and discomfort, and declare your difficulty and uncertainty in communication
- investigate the target culture(s) to establish greater knowledge
- allow time and experience to help

TACTICAL SKILLS: KNOWING WHEN TO, AND WHEN NOT TO

Developing skills (such as analytical skills and communication skills) is one thing. *Applying* these skills at appropriate times and in appropriate ways is quite another — and is a matter of 'tactics'.

As we have seen in previous sections, making sensible decisions about when to apply certain strategies will depend on an understanding of the relative 'costs' and 'benefits'. You don't have to — and can't — learn everything, understand everything, monitor everything, and resolve everything.

This decision-making can apply at both the micro level (at, for example, the level of the individual utterance in an exchange) and at the macro (in making decisions about what aspects of a culture to investigate, for example). These are tactical decisions, which we all have to make in our own way.

More broadly, we all need to have a tactical understanding that the development of skill in intercultural communication is a *process*, and one that never really ceases. There is not a finite set of skills, strategies, awareness, or knowledge that we can learn — and then 'arrive' as a perfectly competent intercultural communicator. As with any life skill, we can all only move forward slowly, setting our individual agendas.

- Successful intercultural communication is about constantly making adjustments.
- Successful intercultural communication is about choosing the critical moments to make adjustments that are *necessary* and *possible*.

INVESTIGATIVE SKILLS

A prerequisite for developing investigative skills is that we have externalisation skills and communication skills.

This is the least difficult of the skill areas, as most of us are competent information gatherers. There is only one underlying awareness requirement —

namely, that cultural variability always potentially exists and is worthy of investigation. A highly ethnocentric attitude, therefore, does not lend itself well to investigative skills. If your way is *the* way — and foreigners either reach your standards or don't — then there's not a lot to investigate!

Most people are delighted to give information about their culture. We are, therefore, surrounded by rich sources of information about any particular culture (as long, of course, as we select the appropriate time and place for such 'research' and choose someone with whom we have enough language in common to pursue the research). Here are just some of the possibilities, with a few words of warning on how the investigation should best proceed:

- Sometimes the 'informant' will be the very person with whom you are already communicating (and with whom you might be having some intercultural confusion).

- Sometimes it's necessary to turn to a third party for your investigations. If this person is available on a regular basis, then you have found that richest of all resources in intercultural communication: a 'mentor'.

- In the absence of either of these alternatives, you can of course observe, always a powerful 'research tool'. You can read — books about the history and culture of the target tribe, newspapers and novels, if these are accessible. Watching television and films from the target culture can also provide useful data.

- Ideally, you need to have a combination of all of the above, checking one source against another. Only with this kind of cross-checking can you really begin to build up an accurate picture of a culture.

People, books, and films are unfortunately not always reliable, either because they fail to capture the diversity within a culture or because they 'prescribe' to you what people in that culture feel they *should* do — rather than what they *actually* do.

- I remember a well-meaning colleague from another culture once giving me some advice which was equivalent to saying something like 'I'm gonna explain something to you — we never use the word "gonna".' Hearing what people feel they *should* do is useful information, but it is not the whole picture!

Equally important when asking questions about a particular culture is to avoid assumptions.

Consider the following questions, all of which contain assumptions directly transferred from the speaker's own culture. How could you rephrase them to avoid (or at least minimise) this?

- How do you say 'older sibling' in your language?

- What kind of gift should I bring the boss on my first day at work?
- I really like the new delivery man. How do you say 'I think you're really handsome' in your language?
- Do teachers get really angry when the kids are late for school?

Generally speaking, these questions contain an ALPHA assumption which you are seeking to transfer or translate ('How do you say...?') into another culture.

The alternative to shoot for is questions that are more open-ended and allow for possible alternatives to your own standard. In the terminology we have adopted, they are X-mode approaches. Also, instead of focusing on 'what people say', they try to get at what people *do*, how they achieve things. This 'functional' approach to communication (see p.59) is potentially more useful.

The alternative set of questions (more likely to be successful and less likely to cause offence or bewilderment) are:

1. 'In my language we have words for "older sibling" and "younger sibling", but not for "brother" and "sister". What's the system in your culture?'
2. 'In my culture we sometimes bring a gift for the boss on the first day at work. Do people here do that too?'
3. 'I really like the new delivery man. Would it be acceptable if I told him I thought he was handsome?'
4. 'Tell me. How do teachers here react when the kids are late for school?'

Look at the following examples of 'information-gathering'. In your opinion, how successful are they?

1. What kind of gift should I take to give the hostess tonight? Do women here appreciate flowers?

Not very successful. It assumes that gift-giving is appropriate and that the gift should be given to the hostess. A more open strategy might be: 'How can I express my thanks to our hosts this evening?'

2. How do you say 'Pleased to meet you' in your language?

Little potential for success. Try something like 'What do people here do when they meet for the first time?'

3. Do you think what I'm wearing is suitable for this evening's reception?

Reasonable potential for success, but it does force the informant into choosing between 'yes' and no'. A more open-ended question might work better: 'How will people be dressed at the reception this evening?'

4. What should I do when I go into the supervisor's office (for our first meeting)?

Good potential for success.

5. At our meeting this afternoon I'd really like to show the chairman how sorry I am that the report is late. How can I do that?

Good potential for success.

6. How do you say 'I'd really like to invite you to my house' in English?

A very risky strategy: It assumes that such invitations are appropriate and welcomed. You need to check the assumption first before worrying about how to say it.

7. Why don't people like to tell you what their salary is?

Little potential for success. It might appear too confronting (after all, if there is a topic constraint in this culture, people may not be enthusiastic about discussing it). Also, it assumes that your conclusion is correct. Instead, try something like: 'It seems to me that people here feel uncomfortable about discussing salaries. Have I got the right impression?' Then allow the person to discuss and analyse the reasons, if they so choose.

8. Do you think the meeting went well?

Again, the problem here is that it forces the person into making a yes/no choice. The more open question, 'How do you think the meeting went?' might elicit more useful information.

9. I've got to do a report for the boss (my first report). Could you tell me what kinds of things are really important for her in reports?

Good potential for success.

10. We'd really like to express our gratitude to your assistant for all his help. What would you recommend?

Good potential for success.

- An English woman, when she first moved to Iran, asked an Iranian how to say 'please'. She was given an unhesitating answer, and proceeded to use the word at the end of all her requests: for example, 'A soda, please'; 'Another one, please'. Unfortunately, the word she was using is used only when inviting people to do things, for example, when gesturing to a chair, or to a door, or to food: 'Please (sit there; walk ahead of me; start eating this food)'. What would her communication sound like using this word with a request?

- When investigating another culture, your questions should not be based on your own culture.

- When investigating another culture, focus on how people *do* things, not on what they say.

How would you go about investigating the following in a particular culture?

- topic choice in informal conversations
- request strategies (using solidarity and deference politeness)
- value systems in 'friendship'
- value systems in staff recruitment

Each of us has highly individual goals in intercultural communication, as well as individual needs, individual concerns, and individual issues that may puzzle (or even irritate) us. It lies outside the scope of this book to address these individual matters.

It lies within your power, however, to address these issues. Each of us can have a 'research agenda' — aiming at better understanding and perhaps better acceptance — by starting with the following basic questions:

1. What I want to know is…
2. What I don't understand is…
3. What really 'gets' me is…

The first of these questions should be straightforward since it aims at knowledge, and should ultimately be achievable, at least to a reasonable degree.

The second question aims at understanding and will require considerable research.

Perhaps the most difficult of the questions on your agenda — and one that ultimately may have no resolution — is the third question, which aims at acceptance. Here, both knowledge and understanding are needed, but a further, rather emotional, dimension is also involved.

Ask yourself what your individual research agenda might be. Consider past difficulties and concerns and future challenges. Of course this agenda will need to be constantly updated.

- Given what you know about intercultural communication, how would you rate yourself as a manager of intercultural communication?

OBSERVATION CHECKLIST
In general, we need to observe our own (and other people's)

- externalisation skills: the ability to step outside usual perceptions
- analytical skills: the ability to figure out what's going on in communication
- monitoring skills: the ability to keep an eye on how things are going in communication
- communication skills: the ability to avoid problems and repair problems
- anxiety management skills: the ability to resolve the emotional aspects of intercultural communication
- tactical skills: the ability to know when to (and when not to) undertake

appropriate action in intercultural communication.

ACTION LIST

- Remember that it is seldom necessary to change your culture, although some modifications may be practical at times.
- Remember that it is not necessary to like the culture(s) we engage with — that's probably not realistic — but a degree of respect is essential.
- Remember that it is not necessarily our aim to accept other cultures, but it is essential to accept that other cultures are valid (at least for their members).
- Accept that it is not necessary to understand everything about the cultures we engage with — a very difficult task for an outsider, anyway. Instead, we need to try to determine which characteristics of a particular culture are the critical ones.
- Remember that the aim is not to become more sensitive, tolerant, and open-minded (although this would not be a bad outcome), but rather to become more *skilled*.
- Realise that your first impressions, your 'gut reactions', are probably highly ethnocentric. Go for a second reaction instead.
- When something is going awry in communication, don't blame the *people* involved. Look for the *problem* — usually a language hitch, a difference in communication style, or a difference in values and expectations.
- Don't make the mistake of thinking that prejudice will disappear if we just 'wish it away'. Reducing prejudice requires the expansion of individual experience, skill, and attitude.
- Stand 'outside' your communication and try to see how it's going.
- Monitor the *gist* of what speakers are saying and, as much as possible, how they are feeling.
- Try to analyse the speakers' perceptions, values, communication styles and strategies.
- Minimise language problems by selecting and structuring your content to match the other person's competence in the language.
- Explicitly state your meaning, your purpose, your intention, your topic, the relevance of your communication to previous utterances, your expectations for the listener, your assumptions, and your value priorities.
- Wherever possible, 'label' what you are doing in your communication and provide relevant background information.
- If necessary, and if possible, declare difficulty with the other person's communication (his speed, his intention, his topic choice).

- If necessary, and if possible, clarify the speaker's meaning, purpose, intention, topic, value priorities, expectations, and relevance to previous communication.
- Repair misunderstandings by making explicit statements
- Provide signals to your listener(s) to show what stage you are up to in your communication.
- Recognise the existence of intercultural anxiety, monitor its development, and analyse its sources.
- Where possible, communicate your anxiety and discomfort, and declare your difficulty and uncertainty in communication.
- Remember that successful intercultural communication is about choosing the critical moments to make adjustments that are *necessary* and *possible*.
- When investigating another culture, don't base your questions on your own culture. Also, try to focus on how people *do* things, not on what they say.

Finally, I hope you have enjoyed this 'journey' through the book and, regardless of your motivation, have many enjoyable and rewarding intercultural 'journeys', whether stationary or mobile.

REFERENCES

Note: For convenience, references are listed by the surname(s) of the author or editor(s) of the relevant publication, details of which are to be found in the 'Select Bibliography'. (In the case of edited collections of articles contributed by a number of authors, only the editor's surname is listed, and therefore does not necessarily indicate authorship.)

Chapter 1
1. Bochner, p. 16.
2. Hall (1966), p. 183.
3. Brick, p. 6.
4. Hall (1984), p. 87.
5. Smark, Peter, *The Sydney Morning Herald*, reprinted in *The Standard*, Hong Kong, 5 May 1993.
6. Triandis and Lambert, p. 296.
7. Tannen, p. 167.

Chapter 2
1. The Human Relations Area Files, initiated by Murdock at Yale University in 1937.
2. Triandis and Lambert, p. 11.
3. Triandis and Lambert, p. 221.
4. *South China Morning Post*, 4 June 1993.
5. Triandis and Lambert, p. 242.
6. Triandis and Lambert, p. 264.
7. Hall (1966), p. 116.
8. Hall (1966), p. 161.
9. Hall (1966), p. 137–63.
10. Personal communication, Professor Bill Foley.
11. Lakoff and Johnson, p. 7.
12. Hall (1984), p. 36.
13. Hall (1984), p. 45.
14. Hall (1984), p. 58.
15. Hall (1984), p. 36.
16. Lakoff and Johnson, p. 4.
17. Triandis and Lambert, p. 45.
18. Serpell, p. 37.
19. Triandis and Lambert, p. 51.
20. Triandis and Lambert, p. 279.
21. Bochner, p. 175.
22. Triandis and Lambert, p. 191.
23. Triandis and Lambert, p. 258.
24. Triandis and Lambert, p. 258.
25. Hall (1983), p. 77.
26. Valdes, p. 96.
27. Hofstede, p. 19.

28. Bochner, p. 73.
29. Serpell, p. 32.
30. Serpell p. 32.
31. Valdes, p. 88.
32. Bochner, p. 73.
33. Hofstede, p. 25.
34. Lado, p. 113.
35. Hofstede, p. 11.
36. Hofstede, p. 93.
37. Hofstede, p. 99.
38. Hofstede, p. 104.
39. Hofstede, p. 106.
40. Hofstede, p. 119 and p. 122.
41. Hofstede, p. 164.
42. Hofstede, p. 165.
43. Hofstede, p. 176 and p. 186.
44. Hofstede, p. 221.
45. Hofstede, p. 213.
46. Hofstede, p. 215.
47. Hofstede, p. 216.
48. Hofstede, p. 222.
49. Hofstede, p. 230, p. 231, p. 238.
50. Hofstede, p. 261.
51. Hofstede, p. 279.
52. Hofstede, pp. 288, 289, 296, 297.
53. Brick, p. 1.
54. Boas, p. 208.

Chapter 3
1. Valdes, p. 73.
2. Valdes, p. 65.
3. Valdes, p. 75.
4. Bochner, p. 65.
5. Blommaert and Verschueren, p. 71.
6. Loveday, p. 178.
7. Loveday, p. 178.
8. Loveday, p. 177.
9. Loveday, p. 177.
10. Loveday, p. 178.
11. Loveday, p. 178.
12. Loveday, p. 175.
13. Loveday, p. 175.
14. Loveday, p. 175.
15. Loveday, p. 175.
16. Loveday, p. 173.

17. Loveday, p. 173.
18. Loveday, p. 181.
19. King (1985), p. 194.
20. Valdes, p. 115.
21. Valdes, p. 115.
22. Valdes, p. 113.
23. Adapted from Brick, p. 121.
24. Hofstede, p. 35.
25. Brislin, p. 152.
26. Brick, p. 107.
27. Loveday, p. 174.
28. Brick, p. 123.
29. Brown and Levinson, p. 62.
30. Brown and Levinson, p. 60.
31. King (1990), p. 176.
32. Richards and Schmidt, p. 182.
33. *South China Morning Post*, 4 June 1994.
34. Hall (1984), p. 63.
35. King (1985), p. 276.
36. Loveday, p. 185.
37. Brick, p. 106.
38. Valdes, p. 14.

Chapter 4
1. Bochner, p. 8.
2. Valdes, p. 102.
3. Bochner, p. 164.
4. Willing, p. 134.
5. Tannen, p. 166.
6. Willing, p. 181.
7. Willing, p. 187.
8. *South China Morning Post*, 14 June 1993.
9. Willing, p. 181.
10. Bochner, p. 171.
11. Bochner, p. 17.

SELECT BIBLIOGRAPHY

Blommaert, Jan and Verschueren, Jef (eds), *Pragmatics & Beyond*, New Series, Vol 6:3, John Benjamins B.V., Amsterdam, 1991.

Boas, Franz, *Anthropology and Modern Life*, Dover Publications, New York, 1986.

Bochner, Stephen (ed), *Cultures in Contact: Studies in Cross-cultural Interaction*, Pergamon, Oxford, 1982.

Brick, Jean, *China: A Handbook in Intercultural Communication*, NCELTR, Sydney, 1991.

Brislin, Richard W., et al, *Intercultural Interactions: A Practical Guide*, Cross-Cultural Research and Methodology Series, Vol 9, SAGE Publications, Beverly Hills, 1986.

Brown, P. and Levinson, S. *Politeness: Some Universals in Language Usage*, Cambridge University Press, Cambridge, 1987.

Hall, Edward T., *The Hidden Dimension: Man's Use of Space in Public and Private*, The Bodley Head Ltd, London, 1966.

Hall, Edward T., *The Dance of Life: The Other Dimension of Time*, Anchor Books, New York, 1984.

Hofstede, Geert, *Culture's Consequences: International Differences in Work-Related Values*, SAGE Publications, Beverly Hills, 1980.

King, Florence, *Confessions of a Failed Southern Lady*, Michael Joseph Ltd., London, 1985.

King, Florence, *WASP: Where is Thy Sting?*, Black Swan, London, 1990.

Lado, Robert, *Linguistics Across Cultures*, University of Michigan Press, Ann Arbor, 1957.

Lakoff, George and Johnson, Mark, *Metaphors We Live By*, University of Chicago Press, Chicago, 1980.

Loveday, Leo, 'Rhetoric Patterns in Conflict:The Sociocultural Relativity of Discourse-Organizing Processes', *Journal of Pragmatics* (1983), 169-190.

Richards, J. and Schmidt, R. (eds), *Language and Communication*, Longman, London, 1983.

Serpell, Robert, *Culture's Influence on Behaviour*, Methuen, London, 1976.

Tannen, Deborah, *That's not what I meant: how conversational style makes or breaks your realtions with others*, Morrow, New York, 1986.

Triandis, Harry C. and Lambert, W.W. (eds), *Handbook of Cross-Cultural Psychology: Vol 1, Perspectives*, Allyn and Bacon, Boston, 1980.

Valdes, Joyce Merrill (ed), *Culture Bound: Bridging the cultural gap in language teaching*, Cambridge University Press, Cambridge, 1986.

Willing, Ken, *Talking it through: clarification and problem-solving in professional work*, NCELTR, Sydney, 1992.

PERMISSIONS

Acknowledgement is made to:

Hofstede, G. *Culture's Consequences: International Differences in Work-Related Values* (Unabridged Edition), 1980, pp. 11, 19, 25, 93, 99, 104, 106, 119, 112, 164, 165, 176, 186, 213, 215, 216, 221, 222, 230, 231, 238, 261, 279, 288, 289, 296, 297. Reprinted by permission of Sage Publications, Inc.

'Life Be In It' campaign, 1981, Commonwealth of Australia coyright reproduced by permission for the cartoon on page 112.

Note: Every effort has been made to trace the copyright owners of material contained in this book. Where the attempt has been unsuccessful, the publishers would be pleased to hear from the author/copyright owner to rectify any omission.